Palgrave Studies in Arab Cinema

Series Editors
Samirah Alkassim
Film and Video Studies
George Mason University
Fairfax, VA, USA

Nezar Andary
College of Humanities and Social Sciences
Zayed University
Abu Dhabi, United Arab Emirates

This series presents new perspectives and intimate analyses of Arab cinema. Providing distinct and unique scholarship, books in the series focus on well-known and new auteurs, historical and contemporary movements, specific films, and significant moments in Arab and North African film history and cultures. The use of multi-disciplinary and documentary methods creates an intimate contact with the diverse cultures and cinematic modes and genres of the Arab world. Primary documents and new interviews with directors and film professionals form a significant part of this series, which views filmmakers as intellectuals in their respective historical, geographic, and cultural contexts. Combining rigorous analysis with material documents and visual evidence, the authors address pertinent issues linking film texts to film studies and other disciplines. In tandem, this series will connect specific books to online access to films and digital material, providing future researchers and students with a hub to explore filmmakers, genres, and subjects in Arab cinema in greater depth, and provoking readers to see new frames of transnational cultures and cinemas.

Series Editors:

Samirah Alkassim is an experimental documentary filmmaker and Assistant Professor of Film Theory at George Mason University. She is the co-editor of the Palgrave Studies in Arab Cinema and her publications include the co-authored book The Cinema of Muhammad Malas (Palgrave, 2018), contributions to Cinema of the Arab World: Contemporary Directions in Theory and Practice (Palgrave, 2020), the Historical Dictionary of Middle Eastern Cinema, 2nd Edition (Rowman and Littlefield, 2020), as well as chapters in Refocus: The Films of Jocelyne Saab (Edinburgh University Press, 2021), Gaza on Screen (forthcoming 2022), and text book Global Horror: Hybridity and Alterity in Transnational Horror Film (Cognella Academic Publishing, forthcoming 2022) which she co-edited with Ziad El-Bayoumi Foty. She is currently writing a book, A Journey of Screens in 21st Century Arab Film and Media (Bloomsbury, forthcoming 2023) and editing a documentary about Jordanian artist Hani Hourani. She holds an MFA in Cinema from San Francisco State University and a BA in English Literature from Oberlin College.

Nezar Andary is Assistant Professor of Film and Literature at Zayed University in the College of Humanities and Sustainability Sciences. He has published literary translations, poetry, and articles on Arab documentary, and researched the relationship of Arab cinema to the recent Arab uprisings. Among his many involvements in Abu Dhabi, he directed a multilingual play for the Abu Dhabi Book Fair and organized an Environmental Documentary Film Series. In addition, he served as Artistic Director for Anasy Documentary Awards in 2010 and Artistic Director for the documentary series Perspectives and Retrospectives in 2013. He holds a PhD from the University of California, Los Angeles and was a Fulbright recipient conducting research in Syria.

Meryem Belkaïd

From Outlaw to Rebel

Oppositional documentaries
in Contemporary Algeria

palgrave
macmillan

Meryem Belkaïd
Bowdoin College
Brunswick, ME, USA

ISSN 2731-4898   ISSN 2731-4901   (electronic)
Palgrave Studies in Arab Cinema
ISBN 978-3-031-19156-5   ISBN 978-3-031-19157-2   (eBook)
https://doi.org/10.1007/978-3-031-19157-2

This Palgrave Macmillan imprint is published by the registered company Springer Nature Switzerland AG.
The registered company address is: Gewerbestrasse 11, 6330 Cham, Switzerland

NOTE ON TRANSCRIPTION AND TRANSLATION

The politics of language in Algeria is complex. Choosing one language over the other can often be overinterpreted or misinterpreted. For names of people and institutions, I chose the transcription in French that usually appears in official Algerian documents besides the Arabic language, and I did not add the Arabic transcription to facilitate the reading.

I used the French titles of the films I mention to facilitate finding them on platforms such as YouTube or Vimeo, when available. These are usually the titles used by the filmmakers themselves. It seemed crucial to me that I use some expressions in Arabic and French to describe social, political, and cultural realities and I did translate them for anglophone readers. The interviews with the filmmakers and producers were conducted mainly in French and in Algerian Arabic; the sections transcribed or paraphrased in this book are my own translation.

ACKNOWLEDGMENTS

My heartfelt thanks to Malek Bensmaïl, Hassen Ferhani, Djamel Kerkar, and Karim Sayad who gave their time for the researching and writing of this book. None of this would have happened without their inspiring films and their help along the way.

This book involved many conversations and exchanges with Marie Chominot, Habiba Djahnine, Nabil Djedouani, Insaf Machta, Narimane Mari, Meriem Medjkane, Walid Sahraoui, and Sofiane Zougar who shared their knowledge of Algerian cinema, ideas, and material with me with a generosity for which I am forever indebted.

I am deeply grateful to Kirk Read who read many (many!) versions of this text and encouraged me at every step. I couldn't have wished for a better friend and mentor.

I thank Julia Boss for her thoughtful editing of a text written in a language that is not my own and that has probably caused her much work while deciphering my ideas.

This book benefited from two research grants that Bowdoin College generously provided.

My thanks go to the members of the Romance Languages and Literatures department and the MENA studies program for their support.

Samirah Alkassim and Nezar Andary's belief in this project from our first discussion to this final book is much appreciated.

A heartfelt thank you to Amina Benhammou, Salah Abbas, Amel Addane, and Ahmed Aggoune who make my sojourns to Algiers so wonderful with their generosity, friendship, and humor.

Special thanks to Oyman Basaran, Yassine Bouzar, Catherine Brun, Mona Chollet, Barbara Elias, Jens Klenner, Nina Kohlmeyer, Sarah Olivier, Géraldine Pinault, Camille Parrish, Arielle Saiber, Lyes Salem, Sebastian Urli, Dharni Vasudevan, and the many friends who found the right words to encourage me or distract me during the periods of doubts.

Lastly, I thank my parents and family who gave me, as always, unconditional support.

CONTENTS

LIST OF FIGURES

CHAPTER 1

Introduction

Algerian cinema is born an outlaw and remained a rebel—
Mouny *Berrah*

We see the village of Ghassira in the Aurès region, where the Algerian War of Independence symbolically started in 1954 and near where the first images of Algerian cinema were shot. Fifty years later, another Algerian filmmaker's camera meanders through a place that seems completely abandoned by the authorities. In one of the village's classrooms, Malek Bensmaïl captures the cheerful faces of young children struggling to answer their teacher's questions about the history of their country. The students can't quite identify which country colonized Algeria and, in addition to France, give several answers as improbable as Mauritania, Spain, Australia, Brazil, and the United States. In this one charged scene, Bensmaïl's iconic documentary, *La Chine est encore loin* (2008), summarizes with humor the disconnect between the official discourse that keeps praising the narrative of the nationalist struggle, and the reality of the inhabitants of contemporary Algeria who appear not all that obsessed by a past glorified and often manipulated by the State.

This book is born from a willingness to explore the meaning and extent of this disconnect without seeing it as a sign of denial or ignorance that can be corrected by a deeper and more lucid analysis of contemporary Algeria, and of the weight of its colonial past. Is it possible to understand Algeria not systematically or exclusively through the lens of its colonial past, without being accused of minimizing its lasting impact? Is there a way to talk about Algeria as a young independent nation, with a focus on

© The Author(s), under exclusive license to Springer Nature Switzerland AG 2023
M. Belkaïd, *From Outlaw to Rebel*, Palgrave Studies in Arab Cinema, https://doi.org/10.1007/978-3-031-19157-2_1

endogenous processes and evolutions? How can one make space for a reality which is crucial, but not always valued academically, politically, or institutionally? If Algerian documentary at its birth aimed to resist colonial rule, what are Bensmaïl and the post-independence generation of documentary makers up against?

The magnitude of the legal, physical, and symbolic violence exercised by the French state to colonize and occupy Algeria has been studied and shown in many works from different disciplines that cannot be fully listed here. Decolonial perspectives such as those developed by historians like Todd Shepard and Françoise Vergès insist on showing that decolonization is an ongoing process and invite us to be wary of a deceptive frame that freezes the colonial violence in the past.[1] Historians such as Malika Rahal, Muriam Halleh Davis, Marnia Lazreg, James MacDougal, and Natalya Vince situate the violence exercised by France within a wider understanding of colonial rule and domination.[2] In her important book, *Le trauma colonial: Une enquête sur les effets psychiques et politiques contemporains de l'oppression coloniale en Algérie*, psychoanalyst Karima Lazali analyzes the enduring psychological impact of colonial violence in contemporary Algeria. Jill Jarvis, in her book *Decolonizing memory. Algeria and the Politics of Testimony*, shows how literature can account for all the losses, massacres, epidemics, and famines that took place during the French colonial rule.[3]

My book, while acknowledging the importance of these works, wishes to step slightly aside by showcasing Algerian film—and more specifically Algerian documentary—and link them to current socio-political realities on the ground in Algeria, thus contributing to a growing body of work on current issues in the Maghreb in general and Algeria in particular. It is, for example, very much aligned with Natalya Vince and Walid Benkhaled's

---

[1] Todd Shepard, *The Invention of Decolonization: The Algerian War and the Remaking of France*. Cornell University Press, 2006; Françoise Vergès, *Le Ventre des femmes: Capitalisme, racialisation, féminisme*. Albin Michel, 2017.

[2] Malika Rahal, "Fused together and Torn Apart: Stories and Violence in Contemporary Algeria," *History and Memory 24*, no.1, spring/summer 2012: 118–151; Muriam Haleh Davis and James McDougall, eds., "The Afterlives of the Algerian revolution," *JADMAG 2*, no.1, June 2014; Marnia Lazreg, *Torture and the Twilight of Empire: From Algiers to Baghdad*. Princeton University Press, 2007; Natalya Vince, *The Algerian War, The Algerian Revolution*. Palgrave Macmillan, 2020.

[3] Jill Jarvis, *Decolonizing Memory. Algeria and the Politics of Testimony*. Duke University Press, 2021.

ongoing project "Generation Independence: A People's History" that explores creative ways to make Algerian post-independence histories visible and audible to wider audiences. They respond to a context where Algerian public history continues to be dominated by retellings of the colonial and anti-colonial nationalist past and where the international lens remains focused on the war of independence.

What if the young children in Malek Bensmaïl film were paradoxically right? What if France were not the key element in an indeed complex equation? What can be said about Algeria and its cultural production when we rely on frameworks that are not forever legible only in relation to France? What understanding of the country can we have when we come back to simple yet nevertheless vital questions: who are the Algerians today? What do their daily lives look like? What languages do they speak? What are their desires, fears, and struggles? What are their beliefs and political dreams? What makes them laugh or cry? Are they that obsessed with France? Where do they come from, and why do they behave as they do? And finally: are they that different from what is revealed in cultural production?

These questions are the ones that have been on my mind for a long time as an Algerian who, even if she lives abroad, still considers herself as an insider, and is active in defending democracy and freedom of speech in Algeria. I am deeply convinced that within the ongoing field of Francophone studies, this perspective can contribute to the understanding of contemporary Algeria without having to constantly link it to France. Algeria has been an under-researched area (in English) and will, I feel, begin to feature increasingly heavily in university courses in the anglophone world. I am hopeful that my diverse personal and professional experience throughout Algeria, Tunisia, France, and the United States and my positionality as an Algerian scholar who studied at a French University and has been teaching for more than eight years in a liberal arts college in the United States of America will provide a capacious and original perspective on my country.

ALGERIAN IDENTITIES

Following the war for independence (1954–1962), the bureaucratic state controlled by Algeria's sole political party the *Front de libération nationale* (FLN) and populated by members of the *Armée de libération nationale* (ALN) manipulated narratives about the Algerian past to construct a mythical version of the nationalist struggle.[4] To serve the party's political ends and create a cohesive national history, the official discourse has omitted stories of internecine struggles deep within the "nationalist family" and sidestepped many crucial aspects of the decolonization process. The FLN's nationalism has thus proved to be a new form of domination after colonization and post-independence. Historian Mohammed Harbi has insisted on the myth of a *peuple homogène* ("homogenous people") and *table rase* ("clean slate") as a creation of the FLN during the nationalist struggle. More recently the psychoanalyst Karima Lazali has insisted also on how pluralism, after the independence, was banned in Algeria—not only political pluralism but also of languages, cultures, and pasts. According to her, accepting democracy would have meant dealing with and organizing a plurality of opinion and identities which the FLN party refused.[5]

The FLN's discourse of unity after 1962 has indeed erased memories and, with those memories, the diversity of the Algerian identity and the challenges faced by Algerian citizens living in marginalized and abandoned territories. The FLN leadership systematically resorted to constructing a mythological understanding of the past that would justify its own power, a myth that rejected the complexity, nuances, and paradoxes of Algerian history. The Algerian quest for an identity that has been attacked and undermined by the colonial ideology has been hindered also by an artificial foreshortening of the country's past and an unconscionable blurring of its present.

Algerian identity is inherently characterized by multiplicity: Amazigh, Arab, Muslim, Ottoman, Francophone, and more. Algerian identities might logically have been expected to emerge in post-colonial formation as marked by a rich profusion of beliefs, practices, and traditions from the Islamic and Greco-Roman-Christian traditions, and by a diverse range of ideas. The colonial trauma, in large part, but also the nationalists' negation of this diversity are among the factors leading to the Civil War that in the 1990s epitomized the struggle to establish the meaning of Algerian national identity. Legends are necessary for building "imagined communities,"[6] but the fabrication of false histories and the imposition of

[4] Mohammed Harbi, *1954. La guerre commence en Algérie*. Éditions Complexe, 1984.

[5] Pierre Daum, "Le monstre dans le placard. La violence des années 1990 et ses conséquences. Interview de Karima Lazali, psychanalyste", in Karima Dirèche (Dir.), *L'Algérie au présent. Entre résistances et changements*. IRMC-Kartala, 2019, p. 271.

[6] Benedict Anderson, *Imagined Communities. Reflections on the Origin and Spread of Nationalism*. Verso, 2002.

a special, invented heroic identity can also be used to justify exclusion and even violence. More dangerously, violence is often promoted through cultivating a sense of inevitability about an allegedly unique and often unflinching identity that citizens are supposed to embody, and which makes extensive demands on them. It is in the context of such fabricated histories that in the 1980s a clandestine and rising Islamist movement aimed to impose Islam as the main—if not indeed the only—attribute of Algerian identity.

This gesture effectively erased other facets of the present and the past, even though the nationalist state had previously embraced erasure.[7] The official discourse of the FLN party after the independence, and especially after the failed attempted coup of Tahar Zbiri against Boumediene in 1967, gave indeed an important place to the *Association des oulémas musulmans algériens* in the person of Ibn Badis and minimized, if not erased, all the other nationalist actors, effectively placing Islam at the center of the nationalist struggle that is often described in history textbooks as a *jihad*. Thus, both the discourse of state authority and the later emerging narrative of the fundamentalists disfigured the heterogeneous culture and identities of Algerians, a process that both generated and maintained ongoing catastrophe. As historian Sophie Bessis shows—and this is true for many Arab countries including Algeria—culturalist and nationalist public policies and speeches giving only visibility to "Islamic modernity" condemned other positions, expressed outside the religious framework, to non-existence.[8]

Major protests began in 1988, especially in Algiers and the nation's other urban centers, and the state answered with a violent repression. The protests nevertheless resulted in a democratic opening. After years of authoritarianism and exclusive governance by the FLN, the constitution was amended, political parties were legalized, and free elections were organized. During that period, 60 political parties were created, and the State recognized the right to freedom of speech and allowed independent and even satirical newspapers, new radio channels, and innovative TV shows. Most importantly, free elections were organized for the first time since independence. The Islamist party, the *Front islamique du salut* (FIS)

[7] James MacDougal, *History and the Culture of Nationalism in Algeria*. Cambridge University Press, 2006, p. 16.

[8] Sophie Bessis, *La Double impasse. L'universel à l'épreuve des fondamentalismes religieux et marchands*. Éditions La découverte, 2014, p. 200.

quickly dominated the Algerian political arena, first by winning local elections in 1990 and then by obtaining the majority of seats in the National Assembly as early as the first round of voting, in December 1991. After the military coup in January 1992 that negated this clear victory by the Islamist political party, a Civil War erupted between the Algerian government and various Islamist rebel groups. Among the many questions at issue in this conflict were those of identity, authority, and legitimacy: who, which group, which institution, which ideology can align itself with power and declare itself entitled to define an Algerian identity?

Debates over the correct terminology to describe this period remain to this day very heated in Algeria. The regime's determined (perhaps even obsessive) wish to control the national conversation about the 1990s was affirmed in the conflict's official naming. The expression "civil war" never appears in official discourse. The dysfunction of labeling is explained by the Algerian regime's refusal to recognize the conflict as having occurred *within the nation*: the Islamists, by nature of their violent opposition to the state and extremism are redefined as non-Algerian. Reinforcing the conflict-era official rhetoric that dehumanized and criminalized the Islamist political opposition—often relying on stereotypes of the terrorist or religious fanatic—vague twenty-first century expressions like *tragédie nationale* (national tragedy) or *décennie noire* (black decade) imply that the tactics deployed by the regime were somehow inevitable and certainly should not be questioned. The regime's defiance toward the expression of "civil war" is an indicator of its unwillingness to address the question of responsibility.[9] Unfortunately, with the official end of the conflict in the 2000s, and the vote of the *Concorde civile pour la paix et la réconciliation* (Civil Concord for Peace and Reconciliation) in 1999, the problems that led to the war weren't addressed and in the absence of trials neither victims nor perpetrators could tell the story of what happened before and during the conflict. Six years later, in 2005 with the *Charte pour la paix et la reconciliation nationale* (Charter for peace and national reconciliation), Bouteflika's regime organized a general amnesty through a judicial acquittal of the terrorists and a financial restitution for the victims, but in the absence of trials, the culpability was diluted. On February 27, 2006, the government went a step further by adopting a decree that gave immunity to all the actors (army, police, and militia included) who used violence during the conflict. Even more importantly, warns the decree, anyone who

[9] Jean-Pierre Filiu, *Algérie, la nouvelle indépendance*. Seuil, 2019, p. 39.

might attempt to instrumentalize the "wounds of the national tragedy" to attack the institutions of the Republic can face a prison sentence from three to five years and a fine of 250.000 DA to 500.000 DA.[10] To borrow an image used by Karima Lazali, it is as if the regime decided to put Algeria's demons in a closet with the risk of letting them grow and come back even stronger to haunt Algerian society.[11] Once again, the Algerian regime opted for a univocal version of the past and imposed it on the nation. This said, it is important to mention that the Civil Concord and National Charter were approved at the time by a large majority of Algerians exhausted by years of a horrendous conflict.[12]

Bouteflika was presented as the "providential man" who brought peace to Algeria, even though his predecessor Liamine Zeroual had already started a process of reconciliation in 1995 with a law of *rahma* (clemency) toward the Islamists.[13] But Bouteflika's presidency, during his four successive terms, was not a rupture with the authoritarian nature of the Algerian regime after the independence. As shown by Thomas Serres, his election in 1999 after the Civil War restored a continuity that links every Algerian president to the War of Independence.[14] Bouteflika kept mentioning his participation in the war of independence—"my generation gave everything[15]"—while silencing the open wounds of the 1990s Civil War. Algeria seemed paralyzed with a regime that drew once again its legitimacy from the war of independence.

In April 2001, Massinissa Garmah, a young man from Tizi Ouzou in the region of Kabylia, died in custody and the protests following his assassination were crushed with more than a hundred protestors dying at the hands of the police, resulting in a crisis within the region that would go on throughout Bouteflika's presidency. But Bouteflika maintained his grip on power, changing the constitution in October 2008 to be able to run for

---

[10] Approximately 1700 to 3400 dollars.

[11] Pierre Daum, "Le monstre dans le placard. La violence des années 1990 et ses conséquences. Interview de Karima Lazali, psychanalyste", in Karima Dirèche (Dir.), *L'Algérie au présent*, p. 271.

[12] The Civil Concord was approved in 1999 by 98.63% of the votes and the National Charter by 97.36 % of the votes in 2005.

[13] Thomas Serres, *L'Algérie face à la catastrophe suspendue. Gérer la crise et blâmer le peuple sous Bouteflika (1999-2014)*. IRMC-Karthala, 2019, p. 58.

[14] Thomas Serres, *L'Algérie face à la catastrophe suspendue*, p. 89.

[15] Abdelaziz Bouteflika, during a speech on May 8th, 2012, commemorating the massacres that happened in several cities in Algeria on May 8, 1945.

more than two terms: he was unsurprisingly elected once again in 2009, with 74.1% of the vote. The burgeoning of social protests and corruption scandals (such as the one related to the businessman Rafik Khalifa in 2007) did not in any way threaten Bouteflika's presidency.

After his reelection in 2014, Bouteflika, who suffered from a stroke in 2013, disappeared from the public eye. His candidacy for a fifth term was announced in February 2019, during a ceremony in which members of his government held a portrait of Bouteflika and offered "the portrait"—a framed painting—as a gift to celebrate the announcement. This ceremony—widely denounced as surreal—and following on years of corruption and authoritarianism—sparked protests, first in the city of Kharrata on February 16. Three days later, in Khenchela, the mayor of the city refused to register the signatures, endorsing candidates other than Bouteflika which sparked a riot. The mayor's office was occupied by protesters who took down a giant portrait of Bouteflika from the municipality wall. Then, after calls spread through social media, thousands of protestors walked peacefully on February 22 in the streets of the capital of Algiers and in cities all over the country.[16]

After years of political anomy and paralysis, protesters chose the word *Hirak* to describe the political movement that began in Algeria in February 2019. The Arabic term *Hirak* comes from the word *haraka*, which means "movement"—thus a way to convey the protesters' willingness to embrace change and to question monolithic discourse. In 2019, the *Hirak* obtained Bouteflika's resignation and the promise that he would not run for a new term. Some politicians and leaders linked to his regime were jailed. The Algerian political system was not, however, changed as deeply as *Hirak* protesters had hoped, and the abstention rate was high for the December 2019 presidential election. After more than a year of consistent protests, the movement was interrupted by the COVID-19 pandemic in March 2020, regaining momentum in February 2021. Subsequently, however, the newly elected president Abdelmadjid Tebboun and his government increasingly engaged in repression of activists and journalists putting an end to the weekly protests. The regime specifically targeted two political entities: the *Mouvement pour l'autodetermination de la Kabylie* (MAK) and the Islamist organization called *Rachad*, both accused of

---

[16] For a chronology of the movement see Omar Benderra, Françoise Gèze, Rafik Lebdjaoui and Salima Mellah (dir.), *Hirak en Algérie. L'invention d'un soulèvement*. La Fabrique éditions, 2020.

manipulating the masses and threatening the integrity and unity of the nation. The regime went as far as accusing the two factions of being behind the wildfires that plagued Algeria during the summer of 2021. [17]

What will become of the movement is hard to predict but scholars and observers now have a better understanding of what it revealed about Algerian society. Peaceful, the *Hirak* was a laboratory for pluralism and non-violent conflict that witnessed a necessary confrontation of ideas, born from plurality of opinions and identities. Many slogans captured the *Hirak* demands to end the FLN's hegemony over the political scene (Fig. 1.1). In Algiers, during one protest on March 22, 2019, I personally saw a student holding Ferhat Abbas's book, *L'indépendance confisquée (The Stolen Independence)*.[18] An important figure of the nationalist movement, Ferhat Abbas explains in this book how the promises of the revolution weren't kept after the independence. The Amazigh flag was spotted in several cities, held by many protesters and when the regime tried in June 2019 to forbid it, the flag appeared even more consistently and oftentimes not held exclusively by activists of the Amazigh cause.

Taken by surprise by the pacifist nature of the movement, the regime used once again the old myth of a "homogenous people" in order to discredit any opposition systematically accused of "endangering national unity." The regime refused pluralism and was unable or unwilling to understand that holding Ferhat Abbas's book or the Amazigh flag was a way for the protesters to insist on alternative, indeed more accurate, discourses of the past. These more inclusive definitions of Algerian identity are still, more than 60 years after independence, contested.

ALGERIAN CINEMA AND NATIONAL IDENTITY

Ranjana Khanna's *Algeria's Cuts* (2008) brilliantly illustrates how high illiteracy rates at the time of Algerian independence and the sheer number of languages spoken in the country would make cinema central to the formation of a cohesive national identity.[19] State-controlled culture played indeed a vital role in the formation of an Algerian national imaginary after

---

[17] Sofiane Orus Boudjema, « Algérie: qui sont le MAK et Rachad, les mouvements accusés d'être derrière les incendies », *Jeune Afrique*, August 20th, 2021.

[18] Ferhat Abbas, *L'indépendance confisquée*. Flammarion, 1984.

[19] Ranjana Khanna, *Algeria's Cuts. Women and Representation, 1830 to the Present*. Stanford University Press, 2008, p. 107.

Fig. 1.1 Protesters in Algiers during the *Hirak* holding a sign that says FLN and *FIN* (the end). Photography by Fethi Sahraoui

Algeria's formal establishment as an independent nation in 1962. The task was for sure daunting, and the new regime was not always up to it. The newly independent Algerian regime was more absorbed in building a homogenous and hegemonic national discourse about the past than creating a nuanced narrative. It sponsored the production of many films that recycled the same stories, images, and footage on the same topic: the unity of the nation around shared traits and a glorious and heroic past in which Algeria sacrificed more than a million martyrs in a supposedly united front. Guy Austin, in his important book on Algerian national cinema of the post-independence era, shows how film works to represent national identities and how the official mythologizing of a national culture has marginalized the diversity of identity that actually exists within the nation.[20]

National cinema, or what many critics call *cinéma moudjahid*, conveys an idealistic nationalism[21] by celebrating the people that become reduced to the "sole hero," as one of the FLN mottos kept repeating: "*un seul héros, le peuple.*" The first films about the Algerian War of Independence and the colonial are a reflection of a glowing, official, nationalist martyrdom. *Le Vent des Aurès* (1967), directed by Mohamed Lakhdar Hamina, tells the story of a mother looking for her son who is held in a detention camp. It was followed by many other movies such as *La Voie* (1968), directed by Mohamed Slim Riad; *L'Opium et le bâton* (1969), by Ahmed Rachedi; and *Patrouille à l'est* (1971), directed by Amar Laskri. *Chroniques des années de braise* (1976), directed by Lakhdar Hamina and winner of a Palme d'Or at the Cannes Festival, is a perfect illustration of this cinema built upon idealistic nationalism, featuring unity and cohesion against all obstacles and heroes with no weaknesses. Although of questionable cinematic quality, the *Chroniques* was probably the most expensive film in the history of Algerian filmmaking,[22] as *cinéma moudjahid* perpetrated a holdup of sorts in Algerian cinema: money was spent generously by the State on celebratory films like the *Chroniques*, while other filmmakers struggled to make films with a critical or even an independent tone.

Algerian sociologist and film critic Mouny Berrah notes that Algerian cinema is also composed of "thematic and aesthetic exceptions (…) that confirm the rule of ideological conformism resulting from the harsh censorship applied to the whole cultural field from the fifties to the eighties.[23]" Some directors managed to make films not aligned with *cinéma moudjahid* and its dominance over the national cinematic imaginary. Some of these filmmakers, such as Mohamed Zinet with *Tahya ya Didou* (1971) or Merzak Allouache whose iconic film *Omar Gatlato* (1979), would know measurable success, offered a resolutely non-heroic depiction of everyday social realities in Algiers in the 1970s, but their films were not

---

[20] Guy Austin, *Algerian National Cinema*. Manchester University Press, 2012, p. X.

[21] Mouny Berrah, Victor Bachy, Mohand Ben Salma et Férid Boughedir (dir.), *CinémAction: Cinémas du Maghreb*, N 14, Spring 198, p. 46.

[22] The film cost a massive two million dollars, while *La Bataille* had cost just $800,000 ten years earlier.

[23] Mouny Berrah, "Algerian Cinema and National Identity," in Alia Arasoughly (dir.), *Screens of life. Critical Film Writing from the Arab World*. World Heritage Press, 1996.

promoted and celebrated by the state. *Tahya ya Didou* was censored and the first screening of *Omar Gatlato* might well have been censored had the authorities not feared the reaction of the crowd waiting to watch it. Films that deviated from the FLN narrative of unity and nationalism would, in fact, be considered anathema in a monopoly of *cinéma moudjahid* that lasted into the 1980s.

The documentary is certainly one of these aesthetic exceptions mentioned by Mouny Berrah. At its birth in Algeria, the national film production was strongly linked to documentary and Algerian cinema, born an outlaw during the war of independence, and remaining in many ways a rebel.[24] Some Algerian filmmakers such as Ahmed Rachedi in the period immediately after independence kept creating documentaries using archival and stock footage. The *Centre National du Cinéma Algérien* (CNCA), newly created in 1963, would support this film and many others, including *Peuple en marche* (1963), directed by Nasr-Eddin Guenifi, Ahmed Rachedi, and René Vautier. On the other hand, sustaining the documentary style and fictional storyline, Jacques Charby would in 1964 direct *Une si jeune paix,* a docu-fiction that tells the story of children who continue to reenact war in their games as they wait out the nation's slow progress toward peace. The young actors in the movie were themselves orphans who had been physically wounded or mutilated during the war for independence.

Despite this first burst of documentary production in the years following independence—and despite continued production of television documentary—creative documentaries would remain rare in post-independence Algeria, and I will discuss this phenomenon in greater depth in Chap. 2. Upon first blush, however, though documentary film had a promising start, and even though documentary could have been an efficient tool for state propaganda, the genre would neither contribute to constructing the national imaginary desired by the FLN nor be able to develop freely under state censorship and state control of the means of production. The situation in Algeria for that matter can be compared to the one in Syria in which film production, distribution, and screening were regulated by the National Film Organization (NFO), established in 1963 as an independent arm of the Ministry of Culture. It adhered systematically to the prevailing ideological mindset of the ruling Ba'ath Party, which came to power after a coup d'état in 1963 and has been in power ever since. As in

---

[24] I am indebted to Berrah for the inspiration for my book's title.

Algeria, censorship on the ground was the rule, and many documentary films were shelved, such as Ussam Mohammad's *Stars of the Day* (1988).[25]

But filmmakers continued exploring the documentary form even when censored. Farouk Beloufa directed *Insurectionnelle* (1972), considered as one of the first attempts to evade the traditional guidelines of historical conceptions imposed by the single-party regime. The film's negative was reedited and screened without mentioning any filmmaker's name. In the more relaxed environment of the 1980s, the colonial past began to be treated with a more innovative tone, notably by Azzedine Meddour in his documentary *Combien je vous aime* (1985), a farcical and satiric black comedy that used music and sound to comic effect over otherwise disturbing archive footage from the colonial period. This film is as far away as possible from the first treatment of stock footage in the post-independence documentaries produced by Vautier, Rachedi, or Guenifi.

In the 1980s, fiction took also over the task of crafting complex narratives. Okacha Touita began working on a quartet of films that would directly confront the myth of national unity during the war of independence, beginning with *Les Sacrifiés* (1982) and then *Le Rescapé* (1986). *Le Cri des hommes* (1990) and *Dans le feu hier et aujourd'hui* (1999) followed in the 1990s. Although *Les Sacrifiés* would be banned because it dealt with the *Mouvement nationaliste algérien* (MNA), a rival to the FLN within the nationalist movement during the war of independence, the film shows some filmmakers' determination to question the myths conveyed via the national cinema and *cinéma moudjahid*. On the other hand, the "Hassan" film series, initiated by Lakhdar Hamina's *Hassan Terro* in 1968,[26] clearly satirizes the dominant myth of the *moudjahid* in Algerian narratives. Hassan is in fact a man who has tried his best to stay away from the battle of Algiers in the 1950s, but later finds himself hiding a *moudjahid*; thus, the false legend of Hassan *terro* (for terrorist) begins. Benamar Bakhti's very successful comedy *Le Clandestin* (1991) similarly questions the monolithic conception of identity promoted by the state and reflects on the diversity of Algerian identity by portraying an eclectic group of travelers packed in an unofficial taxi (*taxi clandestin*). The film doesn't shy away

[25] Stéphanie Van de Peer "The Moderation of Creative Dissidence in Syria: Reem Ali's Documentary Zabad' in Valassopoulos Anastasia, *Arab cultural studies: history, politics and the popular*. Routledge, 2013.

[26] The series includes *L'évasion de Hassan Terro* by Mustapha Badie (1974), *Hassan Taxi* by Mohamed Slim Riad (1982), and concludes with 1988's *Hassan Niya* by Ghaouti Bendeddouche.

from ridiculing the *cinéma moudjahid*: the trip is constantly interrupted by scenes from war movies and images of torture, contrasting with the comedy of the travelers' situation and their conversations in the cab.

With the democratic opening of 1988, as freedom of expression reached the public and political spheres, many filmmakers hoped that the old state practices of control and veiled censorship might fade. But as the confrontation between the state and the Islamists turned violent after an interruption for the elections of 1991, Algerian cinema knew its darkest and most difficult years. The myth of the nation's unity had first been vigorously questioned during the democratic transition that allowed the emergence of new political parties, the return of historical political opponents of the FLN to the country,[27] the expression of cultural claims, and the reaffirmation of a feminist movement. That myth had then been shredded by the conflict that followed the 1991 elections and the sense of horror that conflict evoked in the Algerian consciousness. During the Algerian Civil War of the 1990s, the number of Algerian films in production shrank, as it was almost impossible to direct films during such dangerous times. Despite this challenging context, some works were shot in very difficult conditions of violence, assassinations, and terrorist attacks, including *Bab El Oued City* (1994) by Merzak Alouach, *Youssef, La légende du septième dormant* (1993) by Mohamed Chouikh, and *La montagne de Baya* (1997) by Azzédine Meddour. These three films of the 1990s illustrate a profound reshaping of discourse regarding Algerian identity and a questioning of notions of authority and legitimacy. While their films began to explore the past in ways that could build a new understanding of the Algerian self, violence in Algeria reached unanticipated levels of horror. The late 1990s saw a complete break in film production: for five years, no film crews operated in the country, and all movie theaters were closed except the *Cinémathèque d'Alger*, a public and iconic movie theater of the capital, which remained the only cinema in Algeria to screen films throughout the war.

After the civil war, two opposing tendencies in filmmaking emerged in a country that was seeking peace, with each form competing to establish a dominant narrative for Algeria's national identity. On the one hand—as Salima Tenfiche has framed this antagonism—there is a national cinema

---

[27] In this era, political actors including Ahmed Ben Bella, Président of Algeria from 1963 to 1965, and Hocine Aït Ahmed, founder of the socialist party FFS (*Front des forces socialistes*), came back to Algeria from exile in Europe.

focusing on death, and on the other hand is an independent cinema reaching out to the living.[28] After years of discretion, a propaganda campaign amply financed with state funds had again begun to reclaim the glorious past of the Algerian War of Independence, covering over the horrors of the Civil War.[29] Many of these early twenty-first century state films are biopics portraying "heroes" of the past. While *cinéma moudjahid* of the 1960s and 1970s had celebrated the unity of the Algerian people and their heroism during the war, this new national cinema of propaganda is, as Tenfiche terms it, more a "hagiographic cinema." It celebrates figures of the past, much like the history textbooks approved for the national education system since 1990.[30] *Arezki, l'indigène* by Djamel Bendeddouche (2007) and *Fadhma N'Soumer* by Belkacem Hadjadj (2013) are two films about nineteenth-century colonial Algeria, focused on constructing again a glorious past. Ahmed Rachedi celebrates heroes of the Algerian War of Independence with three FLN-friendly biopics: *Mostefa Ben Boulaïd* (2009), *Krim Belkacem* (2012), *and Lotfi* (2014).[31]

Even if some progress has been made regarding the official discourse promoted by these movies—with, for example, more important space being given to once taboo nationalist actors, women, and the Berber identity—the purpose of this nationalist cinema is still to celebrate the FLN, never deviating too far from the official discourse of unity and of a glorious past. That commitment to the unwavering nationalist narrative likely explains why these films have known little or no success in a country where the imaginaries and myths of unity have been deeply shaken by the Civil War.

In opposition to this nationalist work, a new independent cinema has emerged, financed privately or internationally, focused firmly on the present. Malek Bensmaïl's films such as *La Chine est encore loin* (2008)

---

[28] Salima Tenfiche « Passé glorieux contre mémoire interdite: deux cinémas algériens antagonistes », *Écrire l'histoire*, n 19, 2019, 213–219.

[29] According to Selima Tenfiche, each of these movies had a budget of 1.5 million dollars. *Zabana!* (2012), for example, cost 1.3 million dollars, the equivalent of 150 million Algerian dinars.

[30] See Lydia Aït-Saadi, « L'histoire nationale algérienne à travers ses manuels scolaires d'histoire », in Benoît Falaize, Charles Heimberg, Olivier Loubes, (dir.), *L'Ecole et la Nation. Actes du séminaire scientifique international.* ENS éditions, 2013, pp. 445–453.

[31] *Mostefa Ben Boulaïd* (2009) tells the story of a founding member of the FLN, and *Krim Belkacem* (2012) portrays the wartime experiences of the FLN's historical leaders. *Lotfi* (2014) is about the young colonel Benali Boudghène, also known as Lotfi, who died in 1960 in a battle where FLN forces were far outnumbered by the French colonial forces.

mentioned at the beginning of this introduction are clearly part of this tendency. This independent work either tackles contemporary Algerians' painful memories of the Civil War or represents the profound divisions in a contemporary Algerian society that remains in a state of shock and disarray. Without being completely disillusioned, this oppositional cinema refuses both glorification of the past and idealization of the present. It insists, rather, on what Tariq Teguia, one of the most important and talented of current Algerian filmmakers, calls "recent ruins," himself borrowing that expression from the American photographer Lewis Batz.[32] These traces of a painful and violent recent past are compensated for by use of another image Teguia integrates into one of his short films: *Ferrailles d'attente*, an image referring to the idea of construction still in progress. Specific to the Mediterranean landscape, *ferrailles d'attente* translates as the iron bars on the rooftop of a building under construction (known in construction as rebar), indicating to the viewer that another floor or level is expected soon to be built. This is an apt and poignant image for this independent cinema still under construction, which includes veteran filmmaker Merzak Allouache, who has been very productive over the last decade, with a movie almost every year. Newer filmmakers such as Tariq Teguia, Habiba Djahnine, Malek Bensmaïl, Hassen Ferhani, Djamel Kerkar, Lyes Salem, Karim Moussaoui, Sofia Djama, Amin Sidi Boumediene, and others have followed and built stories that depart from the nationalist and official line and tell of a more capaciously construed Algerian experience and the challenges the country currently faces.

Immersive and Oppositional Documentaries

The filmmakers listed above such as Tariq Teguia, Habiba Djahnine, Malek Bensmaïl, Hassen Ferhani, Djamel Kerkar, Lyes Salem, Karim Moussaoui, Sofia Djama, Amin Sidi Boumediene constitute a new "political generation," in the sense of a group whose political commitment is revealed through their participation as actors or witnesses in a major "generating event," whether political or social, that is no longer exclusively related to independence and the struggles that led to it. This new generation has freed itself, even more than the generation that preceded it, from

---

[32] Bertrand Bacqué and Emmanuel Chicon, "Comme un voleur dans la nuit," Entretien avec Tariq Teguia, February 2019. https://head.hesge.ch/cinema/IMG/pdf/entretien_teguia_bb_ec_v3.pdf/ Accessed June 6, 2022.

the obligation to produce works aligned with any hegemonic or imposed discourse about Algerian identity. Their cinema is no longer constrained by expectations that Algerian identity can be discussed only if filtered through a glorious past. Writing on "national culture," Frantz Fanon argues that "the native intellectual who wishes to create an authentic work of art must realize that the truths of a nation are in the first place its realities."[33] This generation of filmmakers is certainly trying to fulfill Fanon's injunction by conveying knowledge about the lived experiences of diverse, often marginalized, or unseen populations to the viewer.

To speak of identity in a relatively recently autonomous nation is, for this new political generation of filmmakers, to reckon with complexity, ambivalence, and hybridity. This hybridity appears not only through the subject filmed but also through the techniques and modes of representations deployed in the films. Algerian documentaries remain recognizably "observational," while using many of the tactics and devices of other categories of documentaries. Filmmakers often incorporate elements from subgenres supposedly opposed or different from observational cinema. All the films are observational; many tell a story; some are to some extent performative; many convey a poetic tone by stressing visual and acoustic rhythm. With the advent of lightweight cameras and sound equipment, some look on as if camera and crew were not present, drawing from the tradition of direct cinema, as coined by Albert Maysles for the school of documentary filmmaking that first came into vogue around 1960. Others use techniques inherited from *cinéma vérité*[34] whose films are very performative as the sequences are enacted for and by the filmmakers.[35]

This book analyzes the rise of socially and politically engaged documentaries, created in the period immediately following the official end of the Algerian Civil War in 1999.[36] It aims to give visibility to productions that have been overlooked not only in distribution circuits—many Algerian films are relatively unknown outside North Africa, and this is even more true for documentaries—but also within academia. It examines the political significance and the aesthetic power of some of the most influential

---

[33] Frantz Fanon, *The Wretched of the Earth*. Penguin Classics, 2001, p. 224.

[34] Notable proponents of the style include the French directors Jean Rouch and Chris Marker.

[35] Stella Bruzzi, *New Documentary*. Routledge, 2006, p. 154.

[36] Although the violence would not completely stop, the Civil War ended officially with the 1999 Civil Concord referendum; the Algerian parliament adopted an amnesty law on July 8, 1999.

observational documentaries produced since the 2000s. I use case studies to highlight the works of four Algerian filmmakers. In addition to the foundational work of Malek Bensmaïl, I will look at the films of Hassen Ferhani, Djamel Kerkar, and Karim Sayad that are building a more nuanced and complex image of Algeria. For 20 years, these filmmakers have indeed been creating what this book will term "immersive" and "oppositional" documentaries.

I look closely at documentaries whose directors have chosen immersion and observation as a main strategy of formal experimentation in the field of nonfiction filmmaking. They provide a more immediate, intimate, and sensory representation of particular people, territories, and environments. This emphasis on senses and sensory representations led the cinema expert Insaf Machta to coin the expression "aesthetic of immersion[37]" that I find relevant for the Algerian documentaries analyzed in this book. These films' emphasis on the material, physical, affective, and sensory qualities of lived experience suggests that some Algerian filmmakers are interested in conveying a different kind of knowledge, one that is not communicated solely via discourse and clear political statements. The documentary spectator often needs to trust the ability of film to represent reality as a shared experience between director, subject, and spectator; in this kind of documentary making, empathy between the different contributors plays a central role. Empathy is rendered even more possible through an aesthetic of immersion that engages people who watch the film with all their senses.

The documentaries do not necessarily connote completeness. In opposition to the state hegemonic discourse, filmmakers like Ferhani, Kerkar, Bensmaïl, Sayad, and others embrace instability and the idea that nonfiction films are now more likely to be constructed around such arbitrary notions as subjectivity, memory, and uncertainty. They embrace a new form of documentary-making that eschews the didactic function often associated with documentary. The films' dominant aesthetic is *immersive*, as the filmmakers of this century explore spaces and territories with deep attention to detail and equally deep engagement with their subjects and their audience. The films' refusal of voice-over is a strong invitation to the audience to observe and immerse itself in the universe as filmed. These documentaries create a sensory experience through editing and the use of

---

[37] Insaf Machta, « Esthetique de l'immersion de *Babylon* à *The Last of us*», *Nachaz*, April 2017. http://nachaz.org/esthetique-de-limmersion-de-babylon-a-the-last-of-us/. Accessed June 6, 2022.

transitional sequences where not only images but also sound and sometimes even touch and smell are conveyed without extraneous commentary. The films also manifest an exceptional delicacy and gentleness through their composition, the positioning of the filmmaker's own body and gaze among or within their subjects rather than "at" them, and the way an occasional exchange of glances or words evokes a sense of closeness between subject and viewer, and between filmmaker and subject.

I argue that the aesthetic of immersion is highly political. The role and political potential of an immersive documentary is that it represents subjective "realities" and engages people who watch the film in a direct and political way. The power of a good documentary is precisely that it can entice political action and the dissemination of certain social or political ideas. The idea of a shared experience among people affected similarly by certain oppressive discourse and marginalizing events is key. Documentary can therefore secure a more effective interaction from spectators willing to engage with the film on a deep level and to immerse themselves in the reality conveyed in the film. Moreover, the immersive approach is a way to include spectators in the formulation of the interpretation of the film.

The films mentioned in this book are *oppositional* in the sense that they are born out of dissatisfaction with the paradigm of hegemonic discourse and an older, restrictive nationalist definition of Algerian identity. The term oppositional, when applied to their documentaries, implies that these filmmakers challenge, question, and transcend hegemonic discourse, whether national and nationalistic, and also imposed by the West. Their generation has shifted from political silence or discretion to political engagement, while the filmed subjects reclaim their own destiny and craft their own stories as citizens, a right previously confiscated by an authoritarian state that has, so far, ruled over conditions of inequality and injustice. The films often explore a specific place (village, newsroom, slaughterhouse, psychiatric hospital, etc.) or follow a unique character (a politician, an emigrant, a soccer fan, etc.). The documentaries explain, through the words of their protagonists, the possibility of dissidence within Algerian society, a possibility that the protests that began in February 2019 would turn into the reality of the *Hirak* movement. By deconstructing the mechanisms that make the mythological machine of official discourses so effective, these films contribute to the introduction of new languages, techniques, and interpretations into the public sphere.

Documentary can form and evoke change in political opinion if produced with this effect in mind. This book has been informed by a comprehensive view of these directors' output as well as a number of other films from the region; those sources are complemented by numerous interviews, over a period of three years, conducted with many filmmakers to obtain more direct insight about what it has meant for them to choose to work within the documentary form. This book has benefited significantly from my conversations with Malek Bensmaïl, Hassen Ferhani, Djamel Kerkar, and Karim Sayad who consistently impressed me in their shared determination to craft complex and relevant work on modern Algerian citizenship and their hope to convey a broader understanding of Algerian identity.

If the films of these directors are uniformly structured as *oppositional*—delivering alternative stories and narratives—other, so-called aesthetic concerns and serious attention to the cinematic form are also crucial. The documentaries included in this book have thus been selected for their cinematographic qualities as well as their obviously relevant political messages. The formal rigor and elegance of pieces such as *Dans ma tête un rond-point* or *La Chine est encore loin* make them rather unique in Algerian cinema. And while talent is a difficult quality to define, the chapters demonstrate that an engaging and masterful approach to reality-focused documentary may be the most direct route to beauty, even when depicting harsh situations and marginalized territories.

MYTHS ABOUT ALGERIA (AND HOW TO DECONSTRUCT THEM)

In the last 60 years, the Algerian regime has manipulated state-sponsored cinema and national media to impose a mythical vision of a united and heroic Algeria. Meanwhile in the West, when the media spoke about Algeria, and especially during the 1990s, they often eliminated space, time, and personalities, and even more so the political, ethnic, and religious complications and nuances that were shaping events on the ground. The idea that a timeless, troubled, and problematic Arab and Muslim world exists in western minds has been brilliantly demonstrated in the iconic work of Edward Said. In his book *Covering Islam*, Said insists specifically on analyzing American responses to an Islamic world perceived as being more and more important and yet agitated and worrying.[38] The

[38] Edward Said, *Covering Islam: How the Media and the Experts Determine How We See the Rest of the World*. Vintage Books, 1997.

same conclusions can be applied to Algeria. Western assumptions about the country remained static and imprisoned Algerians in clichés: Algerians lack discipline, and violence is inherent to their behaviors; extremism and terrorism are constant threats; Algerian men epitomize brutality, rage, and misogyny, while women and Francophone speakers constitute a progressive force; people from the Kabylia region are democratic, while those from other regions are more conservative.[39]

It is not the purpose of this book to argue that only state-sponsored poor writing or false analyses have been produced about Algeria—this is far from true. I will, however, consider that since the 1990s, most people in the West have been aware of Algeria, if at all, principally as it has been connected to relentlessly monolithic newsworthy issues like civil war, Islamic fundamentalism, and terrorism. Occasions for public discussion of Algeria have almost always coincided with political crises or are obsessed with its relationship with France. It is in fact extremely rare to see writing about the country during its periods of relative calm, writing that would document—either for Algerian or Western readers—the daily lives of Algerians. The overwhelming discursive focus on political crisis and violence in cultural productions about the Algerian people and society, produced either in Algeria or outside, has tended to narrow and fix the range of possible identities and to operate as a form of symbolic violence, ensuring that Algeria is covered over and over by a veil of mystery and fatalism and is repeatedly doomed to political and social paralysis. I do not mean to suggest that a "real" Algeria exists somewhere out there and that both state-funded and global films and media acting from imperfect motives have perverted the global perception of that real Algeria. Algeria cannot be seen only as an ontology. Algeria becomes in this book an occasion for thinking about a different form of knowledge production: documentaries.

Among the purposes of this book is indeed to investigate how representations and misrepresentations can change and be changed over time, in cinema and more precisely in documentaries. The filmmakers discussed in this book are no longer constrained by expectations that Algerian identity can be regarded only through the filters of a glorious and heroic past and established social, religious, regional, and gendered stereotypes. But for

---

[39] Thomas Serres lists many of these myths and questions their validity during the presidency of Abdelaziz Bouteflika in *L'Algérie face à la catastrophe suspendue. Gérer la crise, blâmer le peuple sous Bouteflika (1999-2014)*. Karthala-IRMC, 2019.

these directors, too, the world and the people represented in their documentaries are both objective and subjective entities. They don't hold a monopoly on truth or reality, but their work has contributed significantly to a more nuanced and diverse representation of a country that has often been framed within rigid discourses and most often comes under wider media scrutiny during periods of political crisis.

Criticism on North African fiction films has already looked at dissent through the works of Suzane Gauch, Robert Lang, Armes Roy, and many others.[40] Suzane Gauch analyzes dissidence as expressed through narrative forms closer to entertainment than to the realism of a film like *The Battle of Algiers*. Robert Lang's observations on allegory as an efficient expressive mode in Tunisian cinema could be expanded to many Algerian fiction films. But given that documentary has been neglected in Arab film studies and that documentary has been marginalized in Algerian national cinema is all the more reason to delve deeper into the creative and political relevance of documentaries. It did not escape Viola Shafik, one of the most important specialists of Arab cinema,[41] who has been paying more and more attention to Arab documentary and has just edited a book on the topic with several important contributions on North African and Algerian documentaries. [42] Stephanie Van de Peer dedicated her book to the dissidence of women documentary filmmakers in the Arab world[43] and one chapter analyzes the documentaries of Algerian filmmaker and author Assia Djebar. Laura Marks' *Hanan al-Cinema* (2015) deals with recent experimental Arab filmmaking from the last two decades and analyzes a number of documentary films. Donatella della Ratta's *Shooting a Revolution: Visual Media and Warfare in Syria* (2019) focuses on ways of documenting the events in Syria since 2011. Nicole Beth Wallenbrock in her book *The Franco-Algerian War Through a Twenty-First Century Lens*.

[40] Suzanne Gauch, *Maghreb in Motion. North African Cinema in Nine Movements*. Oxford University Press, 2016 and Robert Lang, *New Tunisian Cinema: Allegories of Resistance*. Columbia University Press, 2014. Roy Armes, *Postcolonial Images. Studies in North African Film*. Indiana University Press, 2005, *New Voices in Arab Cinema*. Indiana University Press, 2015; and Josef Gugler (dir), *Film in the Middle East and North Africa. Creative dissidence*. University of Texas Press, 2011.

[41] Viola Shafik, *Arab Cinema: History and Cultural Identity*. The American University in Cairo Press, 2016.

[42] Viola Shafik (ed.), *Documentary Filmmaking in the Middle East and North Africa*. The American University in Cairo Press, 2022.

[43] Stefanie Van de Peer, *Negotiating Dissidence. The Pioneering Women of Arab Documentary*. Edinburgh University Press, 2017.

Film and History[44] analyzes three documentaries on Algeria but exclusively through the lens of the complex relationship between Algeria and France. Silvia Mascheroni has recently published, in Italian, a book on Algerian women documentary filmmakers in independent Algeria.[45] The relative lack of interest of Francophone academia in non-fiction in the region is striking. As for critics and researchers based in the region, there is an abundance of Arabic publications on Egyptian documentary, but little on other countries in the region. Hady Khalil's book on Tunisian and International Documentary Cinema is less exhaustive than what its title conveys.[46] Hend Haoula, a Tunisian researcher, has published a master's thesis on Tunisian documentary that needs to be completed.[47] As for Algerian documentary, the subject has not yet been analyzed fully in a monograph. I hope that this book which deliberately focuses on Algeria not through the lens of France (all too limited an optic) will contribute to showcasing Algerian documentaries and linking them to current sociopolitical realities on the ground in Algeria. I am aware that the four filmmakers I chose to focus on might not be considered household names and thus dismissed by those who were and are unable to watch their films. But I prefer to take up Bonaventura de Sousa Santos' invitation to explore the inexhaustible wealth of the world and to implore readers to avoid being too comfortable with what they think is worth being studied.[48] My hope is that this book will coincide well with increasing interest among Anglophone academics, students, and others on issues of post-colonial identity and the so-called decolonising the curriculum movement in many US and UK universities.

[44] Nicole Beth Wallenbrock, *The Franco-Algerian War Through a Twenty-First Century Lens. Film and History*, Bloomsbury Academic, 2020.

[45] Silvia Mascheroni, *Memorie. Donne e documentari nell'Algeria indipendente*. Libraccio Editore, 2021.

[46] Hady Khalil, *Al-sinima al-watha'iqiya al-Tunissiya wa-l-'alamiya*. Dar Afaq, 2012.

[47] Henda Haoula, *Esthétique du Documentaire. Le cinéma tunisien post-révolution*, Presses Universitaires de la Manouba, 2017.

[48] Boaventura de Sousa Santos, *Renovar la teoria critica y reinventar la emancipación social (Encuentros en Buenos Aires)*, CLASCO, Buenos Aires, 2006.

CHAPTERS

The chapter following this introduction focuses on the documentary form and its evolution in Algeria. It has become a commonplace to consider that Algerian cinema was born with documentaries during the war of independence to serve that conflict. The genre stayed popular for a few years after the country's independence, but then state-controlled cinema favored fiction. Chapter 3 focuses on Malek Bensmaïl work. With more than ten creative documentaries produced since 1996, Bensmaïl is the filmmaker who has led the way to a revival of the genre in Algerian cinema. Through films like *Aliénations* (2004), *La Chine est encore loin* (2008), and *Contre-pouvoirs* (2015) Bensmaïl opts for an aesthetic of immersion and questions the nationalist official discourse through global narrative that the films tell. Hassen Ferhani, discussed in Chap. 4, chose the documentary form for his two feature films *Fi Rassi rond point* (2015) and *143 Sahara Street* (2019). In these two films, the spectator is invited to enter first a slaughterhouse and then a café. His films convey a sense of closeness and even intimacy with marginalized characters, whose lives will matter much more than any preconceived narrative. Chapter 5 focuses on the work of Dajmel Kerkar who, in 2012, directed a short documentary called *Archipel*, which documents the daily life of two women in a factory. *Attlal* (2017) tackles the difficult subject of the Civil War and explores in the village of Ouled Allal the memory of traumatic events. Karim Sayad is the author of three documentaries: *Babor Casanova* (2015), *Des moutons et des hommes* (2017), and *My English Cousin* (2019). Chapter 6 will discuss these films, and particularly Sayad's use of them to disrupt unexamined assumptions about masculinity and what Algerians would call *radjla*, or successful manhood. Sayed questions preconceived notions about the malevolence of Algerian men, who are often portrayed as the epitome of brutality, rage, misogyny, and extremism.

Returning to Ghassira's classroom filmed by Malek Bensmaïl's film *La Chine est encore loin* (2008) and the students struggling to make sense of what is supposed to be an almost sacred past, the viewer might then understand that the deconstruction of all hegemonic discourses imposed on Algeria is at the core of Bensmaïl's work but also of many documentaries in contemporary Algeria. This long-term work starts with questioning the official nationalist discourse and giving voice to those who are usually silenced and goes on questioning many presupposed ideas about the country, from so-called toxic masculinity to healed traumas. These films do not always constitute a coherent movement, and choices regarding modes of production and aesthetics vary from one filmmaker to the next. I've gathered them in this book for their shared expression of dissidence and the underlying hope for a democratic Algeria.

REFERENCES

Anderson, Benedict. *Imagined Communities. Reflections on the Origin and Spread of Nationalism*. London, New York: Verso, 2002.

Arasoughly, Alia (dir.). *Screens of life. Critical Film Writing from the Arab World*. Quebec: World Heritage Press, 1996.

Armes, Roy. *Postcolonial Images. Studies in North African Film*. Bloomington: Indiana University Press, 2005,

Armes, Roy. *New Voices in Arab Cinema*. Bloomington: Indiana University Press, 2015.

Austin, Guy. *Algerian National Cinema*. Manchester: Manchester University Press, 2012.

Benderra, Omar, Gèze, Françoise, Lebdjaoui, Rafik and Mellah, Salima (dir.). *Hirak en Algérie. L'invention d'un soulèvement*. Paris: La Fabrique éditions, 2020.

Berrah, Mouny, Bachy, Victor, Ben Salma, Mohand, & Boughedir Férid, CinémAction (dir). *Cinémas du Maghreb*. Revue trimestrielle- N 14, Spring 1981.

Bessis, Sophie. *La Double impasse. L'universel à l'épreuve des fondamentalismes religieux et marchand*. Paris: La découverte, 2014.

Bruzzi, Stella. *New Documentary, Second Ed*. London and New York: Routledge, 2006.

Dirèche, Karima (dir.). *L'Algérie au présent. Entre résistances et changements*. Paris, Tunis : IRMC-Kartala, 2019.

Fanon, Frantz. *The Wretched of the Earth*. London: Penguin Classics, 2001.

Filiu, Jean-Pierre. *Algérie, la nouvelle indépendance*. Paris: Seuil, 2019

Gauch, Suzanne. *Maghreb in Motion. North African Cinema in Nine Movements*. Oxford: Oxford University Press, 2016.

Gott, Michael and Thibaut Schilt. *Cinéma-Monde. Decentered Perspectives on Global Filmmaking in French*. Edinburgh: Edinburgh University Press, 2018

Gugler, Josef (dir). *Film in the Middle East and North Africa. Creative dissidence*. Austin: University of Texas Press, 2011.

Haleh Davis, Muriam and James McDougall (eds.). "The Afterlives of the Algerian revolution," *JADMAG 2*, no.1, June 2014.

Haoula, Henda. *Esthétique du Documentaire. Le cinéma tunisien post-révolution*. Tunis : Presses Universitaires de la Manouba, 2017.

Harbi, Mohammed. *1954. La guerre commence en Algérie*. Bruxelles : Éditions Complexe, 1984.

Higbee, Will and Song Hwee Lim, "Concepts of transnational cinema: towards a critical transnationalism in film studies", *Transnational Cinemas 1: 1* (2018): 7-21.

Jarvis, Jill. *Decolonizing Memory. Algeria and the Politics of Testimony*. Durham and London: Duke University Press, 2021.

Khalil, El Hady. Al-sinima al-watha'iqiya al-Tunissiya wa-l-'alamiya, Tunis : Dar Afaq 2012.

Khanna, Ranjana. *Algeria Cuts. Women and Representation, 1830 to the Present*. Stanford: Stanford University Press, 2008.

Lang, Robert. *New Tunisian Cinema: Allegories of Resistance*. New York: Columbia University Press, 2014.

Lazali, Karima, *Le trauma colonial : Une enquête sur les effets psychiques et politiques contemporains de l'oppression coloniale en Algérie*. Paris : La Découverte, 2018.

Lazreg, Marnia. *Torture and the Twilight of Empire: From Algiers to Baghdad*. Princeton: Princeton University Press, 2007

MacDougal, James. *History and the Culture of Nationalism in Algeria*. New York: Cambridge University Press, 2006.

Mascheroni, Silvia. *Memorie. Donne e documentari nell'Algeria indipendente*. Milano: Libraccio Editore, 2021.

Machta, Insaf. « Esthetique de l'immersion de *Babylon* à *The Last of us*», Tunis, *Nachaz*, April 2017.

Mulvey, Laura. "Visual Pleasure and Narrative Cinema", *Screen*, Volume 16, Issue 3, Autumn 1975.

Rahal, Malika. "Fused together and Torn Apart: Stories and Violence in Contemporary Algeria," *History and Memory 24*, no.1, spring/summer 2012: 118-51.

Salmane, Hala and Simon Hartog and David Wilson, *Algerian Cinema*. London; British Film Institute, 1976.

Said, Edward. *Covering Islam: How the Media and the Experts Determine How We See the Rest of the World*. New York: Vintage Books, 1997.

Shafik, Viola. *Arab Cinema: History and Cultural Identity*. Cairo: The American University in Cairo Press, 2016.

Shafik, Viola (ed.). *Documentary Filmmaking in the Middle East and North Africa*. Cairo: The American University in Cairo Press, 2022.

Shepard, Todd. *The Invention of Decolonization: The Algerian War and the Remaking of France*. Ithaca: Cornell University Press, 2006.

Serres, Thomas. *L'Algérie face à la catastrophe suspendue. Gérer la crise, blâmer le peuple sous Bouteflika (1999-2014)*. Paris : Karthala-IRMC, 2019.

Sousa Santos, Boaventura de. *Renovar la teoria critica y reinventar la emancipación social (Encuentros en Buenos Aires)*, Buenos Aires : CLASCO, 2006.

Tenfiche, Salima. "Passé glorieux contre mémoire interdite : deux cinémas algériens antagonistes", *Écrire l'histoire*, 19 | 2019.

Valassopoulos, Anastasia (dir). *Arab cultural studies: history, politics and the popular*, London and New York: Routledge, 2013.

Van de Peer, Stefanie. *Negotiating Dissidence. The Pioneering Women of Arab Documentary*. Edinburgh: Edinburgh University Press, 2017.

Vergès, Françoise. *Le Ventre des femmes: Capitalisme, racialisation, féminisme*. Paris : Albin Michel, 2017.

Vince, Natalya. *The Algerian War, The Algerian Revolution*. Basingstoke: Palgrave Macmillan, 2020.

Wallenbrock, Nicole Beth. *The Franco-Algerian War Through a Twenty-First Century Lens. Film and History*. London: Bloomsbury Academic, 2020.

CHAPTER 2

A Brief History of Documentaries in Algerian Cinema

Le documentaire est le baromètre de la démocratie—Malek Bensmaïl

One day early in my research for this book, I was having coffee in Paris with Hassen Ferhani and Djamel Kerkar. Both are Algerian filmmakers, and later chapters in this book will focus on their respective films. We were discussing the history of Algerian cinema and talking about some of the more influential Algerian documentaries made in recent decades (I was already thinking about this chapter) when Kerkar asked a question that has been on my mind ever since: Why have the Algerian state and the national structures and institutions that fund the arts in Algeria always privileged fiction over documentary? He added—not without irony, since he is a documentary practitioner himself—that the omission was surprising "because documentary can be an efficient form of propaganda." We laughed and then continued our conversation, trying to understand why documentaries have failed to thrive in the national cinema, and especially how the documentary could languish as a form, even as the state and the leaders of public institutions insisted on the educational aspect of Algerian cinema and understood it as a tool.

In fact, as early as 1964, with the *Centre National de Cinéma* (CNC) and the *Office des Actualités Algériennes* (OAA), and in 1968, with the *Office National pour le Commerce et l'industrie Cinématographique* (ONCIC) and The *Centre des Actualités Cinématographiques* (CAC), all

© The Author(s), under exclusive license to Springer Nature Switzerland AG 2023
M. Belkaïd, *From Outlaw to Rebel*, Palgrave Studies in Arab Cinema, https://doi.org/10.1007/978-3-031-19157-2_2

cinematographic activities, including production, distribution, programming, and exhibition were handled by the state. As Mouny Berrah wrote in 1984, the orientation of the Algerian national cinema—as claimed by those in charge of cinematic institutions—has inarguably been one of "educational cinema." [1] That educational label should be understood in the broad sense of a cinema created for the benefit of the Algerian people as, after independence, they collectively grappled with the need to emerge from underdevelopment and the hardships of colonial rule. Algiers, with its dynamic *Cinémathèque* created by the state in January 1965, was throughout the 1960s the hub of Third World cinema. Fernando Solanas and Octavio Getino's Third Cinema Manifesto, which attracted a worldwide following, was well known in cinephile circles in Algiers, and Third Cinema filmmaking practice explicitly favored documentary:

> The cinema known as documentary, with all the vastness that the concept has today, from educational films to the reconstruction of a fact or a historical event, is perhaps the main basis of revolutionary filmmaking. Every image that documents, bears witness to, refutes or deepens the truth of a situation is something more than a film image or purely artistic fact; it becomes something which the System finds indigestible. [2]

If during the Algerian War of Independence documentaries were perceived as a revolutionary tool, competing with colonialism's official narrative, in the years immediately following independence in 1962, Algerian filmmakers did little to exploit the political potential of documentary as Solanas and Getino had theorized. In considering what circumstances might have allowed fiction to flourish more than documentary in national cinema production, Djamel Kerkar, Hassen Ferhani, and I wondered if this orientation toward fiction had in fact been chosen consciously. We pondered whether perhaps this preference for fiction, the neglect of forms like documentary, derived from a long-standing dichotomy between commercialism and critical social commitment. Did the commercial imperatives imposed by the ONCIC, and its officials' rather conservative understanding of cinema, indicate that public institutions privileged fiction because they thought action films and to some extent comedies were

[1] Mouny Berrah, Victor Bachy, Mohand Ben Salma et Férid Boughedir (dir.), *CinémAction: Cinémas du Maghreb*. N 14, Spring 1981, p. 46.

[2] Fernando Solanas and Octavio Getino, "Toward a Third Cinema", http://documentaryisneverneutral.com/words/camasgun.html. Accessed June 6, 2022.

more likely to satisfy the tastes of larger audiences? We surmised that documentary had rapidly been considered as a genre more appropriately screened on television and financed by the public Television and radio channel, la *Radio et télévision algérienne* (RTA), rather than by the ONCIC, which funds nearly all cinematic production in Algeria. And yet, were there perhaps deeper reasons why, in a nascent nation, documentary seemed inadequate, despite its recognized importance as a genre during the recent war of independence?

In the months after this conversation, as I immersed myself in scholarly work about documentary production over the past 30 years, I was struck by the theory of documentary as primarily focused on the complex relationship between reality and representation, with documentary film often seen as a genre that strives for an objective relationship to reality but always fails to realize it. Documentary can never be objective, can never sustain a straightforward relationship between the image and the real. As Stella Bruzzi explains, this missed objectivity has been seen as problematic: "Too often in the past documentary was seen to have failed (or be in imminent danger of failing) because it could not be decontaminated of its representational quality (…)."[3] And yet debates over what reality means, whether reality in fact exists and whether or not documentaries can represent it, were not exactly what I had in mind when I began my work on Algerian documentaries. I had a rather different take on the genre: whatever documentary's relationship to reality, it seemed to me more important to explore the organic relationship between documentary and freedom, and perhaps even documentary and democracy. Much later in my research, during an interview with Malek Bensmaïl, I found this intuition confirmed. Bensmaïl offered that he sees documentaries as a barometer for democracy: "On a scale from one to ten, ten being democracy, I would say that in Algeria today, we are at four. Because even if you manage to overcome all the difficulties related to censorship, even if you obtain permission to film, our films are very rarely distributed and seen in Algeria. Documentaries are indeed a barometer of democracy, and we still have a long road ahead of us."[4] In Bensmaïl's mind, documentaries thrive together with freedom—they are made when the powers that be are not nervous about the truth and competing narratives.

[3] Stella Bruzzi, *New Documentary*. Routledge, 2006, p. 6.
[4] Interview conducted in September 2021. All subsequent quotes from Bensmaïl will be from this interview.

Documentaries may vary in their form, their intent, their treatment of reality, but every documentary brings a fresh and personal eye to events as they take place in a specific setting. When I went back to the simple and straightforward definition of documentary offered by an early practitioner, John Grieson, in the 1930s—that documentary is "the creative treatment of actuality"—I realized that documentary theory often took for granted an idea implicit in that definition. For a filmmaker to be creative with actuality—however "creative" and "actuality" are understood—the filmmaker needs a minimum of leeway and freedom to engage in that creative work. It is with this basic premise in mind that this chapter will tell a brief history of documentaries in Algerian cinema. This is not to sidestep important questions about objectivity, reality, and representation: it is always possible for filmmakers, in whatever the political context they work, to treat reality with more or less honesty, to play with codes, to tell stories through editing, to bring formal innovations, to be close to *cinema direct*—or, on the contrary, to stage and rehearse situations and then present them as natural. But in postcolonial Algeria, it seems of much greater importance to consider the conditions in which this representation of reality—authentic or not—can freely occur.

As mentioned in Chap. 1, the *Front de libération nationale* (FLN) emerged in 1954, and when the colonial regime ended, the FLN became the only party in Algeria. The state monopolized the narrative of the war and its heroes through a film industry that was, until the end of the 1980s, mainly controlled by public institutions. The Algerian government also controlled discourse through tight surveillance of national media and publishing houses. If censorship prevented some films from being distributed and screened at all, then self-censorship must also have played a role: filmmakers avoided submitting documentary film projects, knowing they would receive neither funds nor permission to film. Stephanie Van de Peer correctly states that documentary makers were in this context constantly negotiating dissidence,[5] and that negotiation of dissidence characterized the experiences of both male and female filmmakers in Algeria before the end of the 1980s, even if, as De Peer demonstrates, the challenges for women were greater.

This chapter explains how documentaries in independent Algeria became, over the years, a medium in which filmmakers deconstructed the

---

[5] Stefanie Van de Peer, *Negotiating Dissidence. The Pioneering Women of Arab Documentary.* Edinburgh University Press, 2017.

official discourse and the mechanisms that made the mythological machine of official discourses so effective, by introducing into the public sphere new themes, techniques, meanings, and languages other than the classic Arabic that was until 2016 Algeria's only official language. A description and analysis of documentary's evolution in Algerian cinema should be empirically based, but this account will inevitably be subjective and incomplete, given the lack of reliable official statistics and accessible records of films currently being produced and, perhaps more importantly, of projects censored or refused. This chapter aims nevertheless to explore why Algerian national cinema, which was at its birth closely linked to documentary, gradually abandoned the option. I also hope to show how the documentary would, in Algeria, become the form increasingly preferred by independent filmmakers who did not want to align with the official discourse and instead worked to question it. This overview will not approach the history of documentary in Algeria by compartmentalizing Algerian documentaries into categories defined by different modes of representation. In the non-democratic Algerian context, documentaries are more easily divided between those that are faithful to or respectful of the hegemonic discourse of the FLN heroic narrative (which is not totally false, nor always falsified) and those that are trying to deconstruct it. The majority of the documentaries mentioned in this chapter and in those that follow are creative documentaries or *documentaires de création* meant for cinematic release; only a few were produced by the RTA. As mentioned above, many documentaries are RTA-produced and exclusively screened on television, and those works probably deserve a dedicated study. Several creative documentaries discussed here have circulated on the internet; a very few were commercialized on DVDs; and most are very hard to find. One film, *Insurrectionnelle*, directed by Farouk Beloufa in 1973, continues to haunt me: it was directed by a filmmaker I admire, and I had hoped to include the film in this book, but *Insurrectionnelle* was seen only by a "happy few" and the one and only copy was first shelved, and then destroyed by the authorities.[6]

---

[6] See Mouny Berrah "Algerian cinema and national identity" in Alia Arasoughly, *Screens of life: critical film writing from the Arab world*. World Heritage Press, 1996, pp. 69–70. See also the work of Algerian artist Sofiane Zougar, who retraces the documentary's history in an installation: Sofiane Zougar, "From Insurrectionelle to Libération, installation, tryptic Video/digital print/ Archives," https://www.sofianezouggar.com/works/. Accessed June 6, 2022.

WARTIME DOCUMENTARIES

In its earliest years, Algerian national cinema was strongly linked to documentary: in 1957 a film crew was created to produce images related to the actions of the *Armée de libération nationale* (ALN), and it is a commonplace of Algerian cinema history that it began with documentaries filmed during the war of independence to spur international attention to the Algerian nationalist cause. Like many other Algerian critics and observers, Rachid Boudjedra writes in his book *Naissance du cinéma algérien* that Algerian cinema was spontaneously born in *le maquis*[7] (on the battlefield) with short films conceived to document the war through images that the leaders of the national struggle intended to serve as archives for those who would later write the history of the war. The images were intended for an international audience, but the film crews lacked the means to compete with international broadcasts of the news reports being shot by American television crews. While the Algerian crews produced images that were symbolic rather than realistic and were evidently meant to sway international opinion toward the position that the nationalist struggle was legitimate, we must also keep in mind the difficult—if not deadly—conditions in which these images were produced amid firefights and battles with the French army, with unsophisticated camera equipment, and no capacity to develop the films which were instead sent off to Tunisia and Yugoslavia for processing. This attention to the conditions of filming reminds us that for these early documentary filmmakers, their work was not a matter of artistically transcending or representing reality, but rather of filming what happened in front of their cameras whenever possible. The desire, at least, to erase any subjectivity in the anonymity bestowed upon these films, at least at the time—to any film.

It was in 1957, in the region of Tebessa linked to the *Wilaya 1* (the military district that contained the Aurès mountains), that the first ALN cinema unit was created under the name "Groupe Farid." Farid was the wartime nickname of French filmmaker René Vautier, also known as Farid Dendeni, who had decided to join the FLN during the war of Algerian independence. The group had six members: René Vautier, Djamel Chanderli, Mohamed Guenez, Ali Djenaoui, Ahmed Rachedi, and Mohamed Lakhdar Hamina. In 1958, the unit was given the name *Service du Cinéma National*, attached to the provisional Algerian government or

---

[7] Rachid Boudjedra, *Naissance du cinéma algérien*. Editions François Maspéro, 1971, p. 47.

Governement provisoire de la République algérienne (GPRA) in Tunis, and annexed to the Ministry of Information. The *Service du Cinéma National* constituted the nucleus of the various public organizations that after independence would be responsible for producing films. *Algérie en flammes* (1958) was produced with images filmed in the mountains by René Vautier and Ali Djanaoui.[8] It marks the culmination of the film experience in the "maquis," as most of the group's members were killed or imprisoned not long after.[9] In addition to *Algérie en flammes,* the group produced other documentary films: in *Sakiet Sidi Youcef* (1958), a Tunisian village is filmed after being bombed by the French Army. *Djazairouna* (1959), directed by René Vautier, Djamel-Eddine Chanderli, Mohamed Lakhdar Hamina and Pierre Chaulet, uses footage from "le maquis" to tell the history of Algeria and the nationalist struggle. The film's impact abroad was significant, as it allowed international audiences to see for the first-time images filmed from the nationalist point of view. A year later the documentary was expanded with additional archival footage and renamed *La voix du peuple.* *Les Fusils de la liberté* (1962) directed by Djamel-Eddine Chanderli, Mohamed Lakhdar Hamina and Serge Michel tells the story of an ALN convoy transporting weapons and ammunition from Tunisia to the Algerian desert.[10]

Algerian cinema thus has its roots in short documentaries, emerging from the sheer determination of a group of independence fighters who were only roughly trained in filmmaking.[11] In this earliest incarnation, cinema in Algeria seems quite immediately anchored in the real. Also, worth mentioning in this context is that many of the films produced by the French colonial administration in the same place and time were also documentaries: more than 130 French documentary films produced between 1946 and 1954 were clearly intended to showcase the positive achievements of colonial rule in Algeria.[12] And yet, despite Algerian cine-

---

[8] *Algérie en flammes* (1958) is included in the DVD: *René Vautier en Algérie. 15 films de René Vautier. 1954-1988,* Les Mutins de Pangée, 2014.

[9] Lotfi Meherzi, *Le cinéma algérien: institutions, imaginaire, idéologie.* SNED, 1980, p. 63.

[10] Benjamin Stora, « Le cinéma algérien entre deux guerres », *Confluences Méditerranée,* No. 81 (Feb. 2012): 181–188.

[11] For a detailed account on the cinematic representations of the Algerian War of Independence see Ahmed Bedjaoui, *Cinéma et guerre de libération. Algérie, des batailles d'images.* Chihab, 2014.

[12] Sébastien Denis, *Le Cinéma et la guerre d'Algérie: la propagande à l'écran (1945-1962).* Nouveau Monde éditions, 2009, pp. 75–92.

ma's indisputable documentary origins, documentary filmmaking would gradually lose momentum in the years following independence.

Documentaries in the 1960s

After independence, the new state created several different organizations with responsibility over the production of films. The ONCIC took over in 1968 and maintained a monopoly of film distribution and production until the late 1980s.[13] Some of those involved in these organizations—including René Vautier, Ahmed Rachedi, and Mohammed Lakhdar Hamina—had participated in the ALN cinema unit, and the latter would become an important and rather controversial figure in the years following the end of French colonization. As Patricia Caillé has shown, "Algerian cinema" in the years following independence was an "all-encompassing term," [14] with a stated purpose of educating the masses. The institutions created to support it were numerous and varied: the *Centre audio-visuel de Ben Aknoun* (Audiovisual Center of Ben Aknoun), the *Office des actualités algériennes* (the Office of Algerian Newsreel), and the private production company Casbah Films were just a few among the organizations created under the state's broad cinematic umbrella. Their missions differed considerably as well, and I mention these three in particular because of their respective roles in the evolution of documentary in Algeria. The *Radio et télévision algérienne* (RTA) (The National Radio and Television Channel) should be mentioned as well, as it also produced many documentary films shot in 16 mm. Their crews were Algerian, their production costs were lower, and the administrative and technical constraints for filmmakers were fewer.

The Centre Audio-Visuel De Ben Aknoun

The Algiers Audiovisual Center is the main organ of the *Fédération algérienne du cinéma populaire* (FACP), which operates under the supervision of the Ministry of Youth, Sports and Tourism. René Vautier and Ahmed

---

[13] For a detailed account of the institutions dedicated to cinema see Hala Salmane, Simon Hartog and David Wilson, *Algerian Cinema*. British Film Institute, 1976 and Wassyla Tamzali, *En attendant Omar Gatlato*. ENAP, 1979.

[14] Patricia Caillé, « On the Shifting Significance of 'Algerian Cinema' as a Category of Analysis, in Rabah Aissaoui and Claire Eldridge (ed.), *Algeria revisited: history, culture and identity*. Bloomsbury, 2017, p. 161.

Rachedi created the center in the spring of 1962, hoping to produce movies on a limited budget and contribute to the emergence of a free and popular national cinema. The center's motto was: "Towards socialism through cinema, beyond all censorship," and the organizers invited Algerian filmmakers to express themselves in an unconstrained investigation of the issues the country would face in its march towards socialism. The initiative aligned with the "democratic and popular options" the FLN had outlined during its Congress in Tripoli in June 1962 and reiterated in the Algiers Charter adopted in April 1964. According to the charter, cultural production in Algeria was to serve the revolution.[15]

The documentary genre was the form preferred by Vautier and Rachedi, and the members of the center directed a series of *reportages* on the situation in the country during the first months after independence. *Un seul acteur le peuple* (1962) films the celebration of International Labor Day on May 1, and the center's most important work, the documentary *Peuple en marche* (1963)—directed by Nasr-Eddin Guenifi, Ahmed Rachedi, René Vautier and others[16]—is similarly focused on the collective work of building a postcolonial society. *Peuple en marche*, which can be considered the first feature documentary produced in independent Algeria, retraces the history of the war and shows the popular effort to rebuild. Under the patronage of René Vautier, the filmmakers reuse footage from *Algérie en flammes* (1958), mentioned above. They evoke the past and focus their cameras on the present and the future they dream of for the nation. The film's opening sequence shows two cameras on a helicopter filming the city of Algiers from the sky before descending into the streets of the city. The voice of the commentary announces the filmmakers' intentions: *je dis ce que je vois, ce que je sais, ce qui est vrai*, "I say what I see, what I know, what is true." The film is then divided into two parts of almost equal length, one dedicated to the past and the war and the other dedicated to the present and the country's (re)construction. The film is aligned with the official discourse and political orientations of President Ben Bella's socialist regime and was screened primarily through the network known as the *ciné-pop*, short for *Cinémas populaires*. Created by he Algerian

[15] *La Charte d'Alger. Ensemble des textes adoptés par le 1er Congrès du Parti du Front de libération nationale (du 16 au 21 avril 1964)*. Commission Centrale d'Orientation du FLN, (Alger), 1964. 176 pp.

[16] *Peuple en marche*, is included on the DVD *René Vautier en Algérie. 15 films de René Vautier. 1954-1988*, Les Mutins de Pangée, 2014.

Federation of Popular Cinema, the *ciné pop* were venues for film screening and education, created to train viewers in cinematographic language, using film to invite debate on current social and political issues.[17]

After Boumediene acceded to power in Algeria following the military coup of 1965, *Peuple en marche* was banned, because the film's second half mentioned Ben Bella's achievements and the Boumediene government would not tolerate the celebration of the man they had just ousted. This censorship of *Peuple en marche* was motivated by this specific aspect of the film and underscores that censors would step in whenever a film failed to align with the ruling power's official version of events. The year before he left Algeria for France in 1966, René Vautier also collaborated with Algerian author Mammeri to write *L'Aube des damnés* (1965), a documentary about the history of colonization and the anticolonial struggles, which would be directed by Ahmed Rachedi and produced by the newly constituted CNC.

The Office of Algerian Newsreel (L'Office des actualités algériennes, OAA)

The *Office des actualités algériennes* (OAA) was created by Mohamed Lakhdar Hamina and directed by Pierre Clément. Like René Vautier and Ahmed Rachedi, Lakhdar Hamina and Clément had belonged to the ALN cinema unit. The office's mission was to produce, under the supervision of the ministry of information, didactic short films and newsreels to be projected in movie theaters across the country. The films drew large audiences between 1963 and 1964 with shorts about literacy, hygiene, and health, almost all of them directed by Lakhdar Hamina. *La promesse de juillet* (1963) addresses the first steps in the national experience of self-rule; *Une fois de plus* (1963) is about the campaign for the *Fonds de solidarité* (National fund for solidarity) and *Lebeick Pierre noire* (1963) is about the pilgrimage to Mecca. But Mohamed Lakhdar Hamina transformed the Office into a production and distribution house that produced fiction films rather than the documentaries that would seem to be more logically aligned with the Office's initial mission. In 1964, the office released its

---

[17]Sébastien Layerle, « Premières images de l'Algérie indépendante: *Un peuple en marche* (1964) ou « l'épopée » du Centre audiovisuel d'Alger », *Décadrages* [On line], 29-30 | 2016, last accessed May 2019. URL: http://journals.openedition.org/decadrages/794. DOI: 10.4000/ decadrages.794.

first short fiction film—*Le Temps d'une image* (1964)—and then between 1963 and 1974, the OAA went on to produce or co-produce approximately ten fiction films. The best known of these are *Décembre* (1972), directed by Lakhdar Hamina, and *Les remparts d'argile* (1970), directed by Jean-Louis Bertucelli.

Casbah Film

As the sole private production house to emerge in the newly independent Algeria—which had officially opted to nationalize its cinema in August 1964—Casbah Film likewise participated in the pivot away from documentary in the postwar years. Casbah Film is known to be closely tied to the personal experience of its founder, Yacef Saadi, who fought in the Algerian War of Independence and was an FLN military commander for the Autonomous Zone of Algiers during what historians call the Battle of Algiers (1956–1957). That he could sustain his exceptional private producer status likely derives from his participation in this iconic event and from his close relationship to President Ben Bella. The company was organized on a for-profit model and had a large budget. As Rachid Boudjedra has noted, Casbah Film intended to produce commercial films that would have an impact in Algeria and abroad. The company's first film was a documentary, *Les mains libres* (1964), directed by Italian filmmaker Ennio Lorenzini.[18] Another early film was the iconic *La Bataille d'Alger* (1967). Scholars including David Forgacas and Algerian directors Malek Bensmaïl and Cheikh Djemaï have told the story of this film and described the role played by the *Front de libération nationale* (FLN) military commander Yacef Saadi and his production company Casbah Film in making this film possible. Yacef Saadi played Djafar, a fictionalized version of himself, at the suggestion of the Italian filmmaker Gillo Pontecorvo and the film is, in fact, based on Saadi's memoir, *Souvenirs de la bataille d'Alger,* and was backed by Casbah Films.[19] Worth noting further here is that the film was deeply rooted in the documentary genre. Before reaching out to Pontecorvo, as a former member of the Italian Communist Party who had

---

[18] About the documentary *Les mains libres,* see the work of artist Zineb Sedira during the Venice Biennale 2022. After 1966, *Les Mains Libres* was lost, Sedira eventually found the forgotten work in a small archive in Rome. See https://www.zinebsedira.com . Accessed June 6, 2022.

[19] David Forgacs, "Italians in Algiers," *Interventions.* Vol. 9, n. 3, 2007, pp. 350–364 and Cheikh Djemai, *La Bataille d'Alger, l'empreinte,* 2018.

been part of the Italian resistance to fascism, Saadi had begun the project by writing a treatment with René Vautier. The Audiovisual Center team interviewed actual casbah residents who had lived through or participated in the "Battle of Algiers" and then drew on those interviews to write the screenplay for what would become Pontecorvo's eponymous film. The Italian filmmaker ultimately opted for the realist film style of the documentary newsreel, using location shooting, grainy black and white photography, and frequent hand-held camerawork, techniques that are clearly inspired by documentary. *The Battle of Algiers* (1967) would set the tone for Algerian cinema for decades to come, and its release seems to coincide with the transition moment Djamel Kerkar observed above, after which Algerian filmmakers would typically choose the path toward fiction.

Also released in 1967 was the important documentary *Elles*, directed by Ahmed Lallem and produced by the CNC, newly created by decree in March 1967. Lallem had worked as a war reporter on the Algerian-Tunisian border and then trained with Yugoslavian television in Belgrade and pursued filmmaking studies in Poland and France. For *Elles* (1967), he worked with Sarah Maldoror as assistant director.[20] Together they filmed teenage Algerian girls who attended the Ourida Meddad girls high school in the neighborhood of El Harrach, talking to them about their hopes and desires for the nascent country. Lallem films discussions between the high school girls as well as comments from several teachers on the state of women's rights in Algeria. Maldoror and Lallem adopt a *cinéma verité* perspective, allowing the spectator to see frequent rebuttals from the instructors, knowing sidelong glances between students, and life on the street outside the school as it reflects the substance of the girls' comments. Their discussions remain unresolved. *Elles* is probably the first documentary filmed in postcolonial Algeria to illustrate the genre's potential oppositional power, but the film was screened only at *La Cinémathèque d'Alger* and unlike many other documentaries and films produced in the period, would not see national distribution.

During the Pan African Festival of 1969, American filmmaker William Klein directed a documentary about the festival, recording details of a period often viewed as epitomizing Algiers's willingness to serve as the

---

[20] Sarah Moldoror, a French filmmaker of French West Indian descent, also travelled to Algiers to direct a short film, *Monangambeee* (1969) about the Angolan anticolonial struggle; Algerian filmmaker Mohammed Zinet appears as an actor in that film.

"Mecca of revolutions."[21] And even though the documentary form praised in the Solanas and Getino manifesto did not generally thrive in Algeria, new-generation documentary filmmakers like Hassen Ferhani and Nabil Djedouani would later come to know the work of directors like Klein. As we will see in Chap. 3, when Ferhani and Djedouani decided to film the second Pan African Festival in 2009, partly as an homage to Klein's project, they demonstrate that the films of the 1960s have had a lasting impact on documentary filmmaking in Algeria.

The *Centre audiovisuel* disappeared after René Vautier left Algeria in 1966, when the *Office des actualités algériennes* terminated its initial mission of producing newsreels. It was then incorporated into the ONCIC allowing the Boumediene regime to assume an ever-greater role in controlling cultural production. As a consequence, the documentary genre ceased to flourish in Algeria. Fiction would dominate cinematographic production for at least the next two decades. Realism and the realist aesthetic—largely dictated by official policy—would replace the documentary perspective, and yet would fail to obtain any authenticity. Instead, as Viola Shafik has argued, that Algerian realism has devoted itself to presenting a clear cut, often negative, view of reality while demanding the realization of utopia, thus imprinting its "revolutionary" political ideals on reality.[22]

DOCUMENTARY, CENSORSHIP, AND DISSIDENCE IN THE 1970S AND THE 1980S

The decade of the 1970s was a high point in the volume of film production in Algeria: on average, two or three entirely Algerian-produced films were released each year, with a peak of nine films released in 1972 and five in 1978. But as early as 1964, Algerian censorship mechanisms were firmly in place; any shooting in the country took place under the systematic control of national authorities. Censorship was initially managed by the CNC and beginning in August 1964 authorization from the ministry of information would be required for anyone wishing to film inside Algerian borders. From November 1964 on, the process would be further reinforced by a newly created literary and artistic commission, with a more formal

---

[21] The expression, widely used in the 1960s, was recently revived by Jeffrey James Byrne as the title of his book *Mecca of Revolution: Algeria, Decolonization, and the Third World Order.* Oxford University Press, 2016.

[22] Viola Shafik, *Arab Cinema. History and Cultural Identity.* AUC Press, 1997, p. 154.

layer added in March 1967, in the form of a national commission on censorship.[23] Censorship was from then on official state policy, and the commission would be further charged with assuring that the content of films
produced in Algeria be consistent with the socialist orientation and the
guidelines on foreign affairs established by the National Charter. The ministry of information had the power to stop a film project. Moreover, since
no private production companies existed at the time—except for Casbah
Film—filmmakers hoping to see their projects qualify for funding and production assistance faced strong incentives to self-censor.[24] The ministry
exercised systematic control over films, intervening at even the very early
stages of conception, to the extent that in the early 1970s some filmmakers complained of the excessive oversight in a common manifesto they
presented to the ministry of information.[25] Meherzi, in his 1980 study of
Algerian cinema, attempted to articulate the criteria according to which
films were accepted or rejected, revealing that no written policy established explicit rules for censors or filmmakers to follow.[26] Meherzi and
Boudjedra have both identified the National Charter as the central text
guiding the members of the commission, but the charter's principles and
framing concepts are vague, and much would remain open to personal
interpretation when it came to judging scripts or storylines. Because the
commission was tasked with maintaining "Arab-Muslim customs," "public order," and "good morals," and was to prohibit "things that do not
correspond to what is commonly accepted and embarrass the audience,"
the laws of censorship were effectively turned into "unpredictable official
weapons."[27]

If it is hard to know the number of documentaries (or, for that matter,
the number of fiction films) that were censored in the early stages of their
conceptualization, we do know of two important films that were censored
after their production. Both were commissioned by official authorities,
and both seem to have disappointed those authorities' expectations. The
first film is *Tahya ya Didou*, directed by Mohamed Zinet in 1971. Zinet
was assistant director to Ennio Lorenzini on the documentary *Les Mains*

[23] Lotfi Meherzi, *Le cinéma algérien: institutions, imaginaire, idéologie.* SNED,
1980, p. 207.

[24] Viola Shafik, *Arab Cinema.* p. 36.

[25] Hala Salmane, Simon Hartog, David Wilson, *Algerian Cinema*, British Film Institute,
1976, p. 41.

[26] Lotfi Meherzi, *Le cinéma algérien.* 1980.

[27] Viola Shafik, *Arab Cinema.* p. 36.

libres (1964) and to Gillo Pontercorvo on *La Bataille d'Alger* (1966). The City of Algiers commissioned the film from Zinet and supplied funding, but Zinet's film was rejected on completion and was never given a proper cinematic release. As Guy Austin has observed, *Tahya ya Didou* occupies a pivotal position between fiction and documentary.[28] It uses performed sequences and *cinéma vérité* footage of the Casbah. The storyline follows a tourist couple as they wander through the city of Algiers. The man had served in the French army during the war of Algerian independence; now, returning to Algiers, he encounters a blind man and realizes that he had tortured him during his army service. The film is punctuated with sequences in which a poet named Momo delivers verses, an elegy to Algiers. It ridicules the FLN's rituals of triumphalism in a sequence where a ceremony in a sports stadium is interrupted by a woman screaming. The film depicts a society caught between tradition and modernity: it shows the modernization of the Boumediene era, while also capturing traces of a traditional society, and reflecting on the aftermath of historical trauma. The city of Algiers is not celebrated, but is instead shown with all its contrasts, contradictions, and challenges. The commissioning authorities detested Zinet's vision of the city, and the film was shelved. Was it only the mayor of Algiers, who bore the production costs of the commissioned work, who disapproved of the film? Was it that the film didn't fit with the ideology of the period? Was the film insufficiently celebratory and in some sense too close to reality in its *cinéma verité* approach? Was it the film's distinctive aesthetic quality that dismayed the commission? Little is known about why the film was rejected, but we do know that there was never a general release—and that Zinet was never able to secure funding for a second film. A poor-quality version of the original film is available on YouTube, and the film was restored in 2017 by Laser Film, an Italian company. The restored version was screened in Marseille in July 2021 during the International Film Festival (FID), and Hassen Ferhani managed to obtain a copy of the film from for a screening at the Swiss festival *Visions du réel*, in April 2022, but as of this writing it has not yet been screened in Algeria. *Tahya ya Didou* is now considered one of the masterpieces of Algerian cinema. In the 1970s, its experimental approach was innovative, blending fiction and documentary, and the film later inspired many Algerian filmmakers, including Merzak Allouache and Assia Djebar.

---

[28] Guy Austin, *Algerian National Cinema*. Manchester University Press, 2012, p. 56.

Another documentary censored and rejected on completion is one that Farouk Beloufa and Yazid Khodja directed at approximately the same time as Zinet's filming of *Tahya Ya Didou*. This second film was commissioned by the audiovisual services of the Ministry of Information and was intended as a response to the French documentary *La guerre d'Algérie* (1972), directed by Yves Courière and Philippe Mounier. Algerian authorities deemed the French film biased and considered it a falsification of the past: a new documentary, this time produced by Algeria and directed by Algerians,[29] would respond to the French narrative. The first major production of Farouk Beloufa, the Algerian documentary *Insurrectionnelle* was completed in 1973.[30] Censors rejected the first version. October 1974 saw the release of a completely reedited version of the film's 90 minutes of content. Algerian authorities presented it in theaters as a collective work, without signature, under the title *La Guerre de Libération*. According to Beloufa, the original copy was destroyed, so few have seen the documentary in its initial form; as a result it is difficult to reconstruct why the commissioning authorities were dissatisfied. Maherzi in his book quotes extensively from articles published in *El Djeich*, the official newspaper of the Algerian army (ALN), which criticizes the censorship of the film and ridicules the final version as caricatural. Maherzi says authorities disapproved of Beloufa's (supposedly Marxist) interpretation of the past. As with *Tahya ya Didou*, we can assume that the reasons for censorship were ideological, a failure to align the film's message with the dominant discourse. In the three years from 1971 to 1973, then, we see both a documentary and an experimental film—operating between fiction and documentary—both commissioned by the authorities and then both censored after the fact.

As Mouny Berah observes, many important issues such as language, love, sexuality, and religion, and the question of women on screen were aired in documentaries. "But the experience of *Insurrectionnelle* (1972) by Farouk Beloufa, and *Combien je vous aime* (1982) by Azzedine Meddour, are proof that censorship was constantly expanding its field of operations."[31] Although they are rare, and it was hard to get them pro-

---

[29] Lotfi Meherzi, *Le Cinéma algérien*. 1980, p. 370.

[30] Fahim Djebara, "Cinéma: Farouk Beloufa, l'image manquante de l'Algérie », in *Le Monde*, April 19th 2018. https://www.lemonde.fr/afrique/article/2018/04/19/cinema-farouk-beloufa-l-image-manquante-de-l-algerie_5287758_3212.html.

[31] Mouny Berrah "Algerian cinema and national identity" in Alia Arasoughly, *Screens of life: critical film writing from the Arab world*. World Heritage Press, 1996, p. 66.

duced, the documentaries that were made in Algeria during the 1970s and 1980s were clearly engaged in negotiating with implicit aesthetic and ideological norms; these films questioned the national official narrative of a heroic struggle against the colonizer. Inspired by the work of Mohamed Zinet, Assia Djebar saw the potential for cinema to question the national narrative of unity, as she has continually done in her writing. Djebar directed two documentaries: *La Nouba des femmes du Mont Chenoua* (1978) and *La Zerda ou les chants de l'oubli* (1982), the latter co-written with Algerian author Malek Alloula.[32] Djebar was the first woman director in Algeria and her two films are frequently read as feminist manifestos; they offer narratives alternative to a highly masculine and glorified representation of the past, as Djebar refuses to assimilate an aesthetic standard of heroism. In *La Nouba* (1978), she opts for a personal approach, choosing to work in her native region of Mont Chenoua and interviewing local women including members of her own family. For this film, Djebar opts for a hybrid form between documentary and art cinema, and through that form she gives voice to women who have long been ignored and silenced. *La Zerda* (1982) is a compilation of archival clips with a soundtrack built around multiple male and female voices: songs, poems, whispers, and screams. In the words of Algerian filmmaker Habiba Djahnine, the film "responds to a yearning to bring an inner gaze to what has befallen our sacred memory by relying on archival footage so as to reveal the ferocity of that which African peoples and lands endured.[33]" The film has the audacity to look beyond the masculine heroism and unity of the official narrative of the war and to craft instead an intimate account of the past, trying to convey through its images and its soundtrack what women do when men go to war. Djebar knew that even if the films were produced with *Radio Télévision Algerienne* (RTA) they would not be able to reach a wide audience. And if both films were standouts internationally—at the Venice Film Festival and the Berlin Film Festival—they were far from being celebrated in Algeria. *La Nouba* (1978), for example, was screened only once on domestic television and Djebar abandoned filmmaking after completing her second documentary in 1982. In the documentary

---

[32] *La Nouba* is available on Youtube and *La Zerda* is on the DVD *Specters of Freedom. Cinema and Decolonization*, 2018.

[33] Habiba Djahnine, "Des regards libres du cinéma algérien. Uncovered Eyes of Algerian Cinema. A conversation on *La Zerda* et les Chants de l'oubli and *Monangambeee*, in *Specters of Freedom. Cinema and Decolonization*, [DVD booklet], Arsenal, 2018, p. 28.

Barberousse mes soeurs (1985), Hassan Bouabdallah films former women emprisonned in the prison of Barberousse, during the Algerian War of Independence, reacting to a fiction film *Barberouuse* (1982), directed by Hadj Rahim. The documentary works as an efficient way to nuance the masculine heroism of the fiction and of the official narrative.

When private production companies were allowed into Algeria a few years later, as the country experienced its first period of democratic opening, Assia Djebar would lend her voice to Merzak Allouache for his documentary *Femmes en movement* (1989), reading a narrative about women and their fight for equal rights in Algeria. *Femmes en movement* is one of two documentaries that Merzak Allouache directed during the period of hope and turmoil that followed the democratic opening of 1989. *Femmes en movement* focuses more closely on the feminist movement, while *L'après Octobre* (1988) investigates the broader cultural, social, and political changes Algeria was witnessing at the time. As discussed in the introduction, Allouache had already questioned the triumphant national discourse in his first movie *Omar Gatlato* (1976), and the trajectory of his cinematic career speaks eloquently to the fact that documentaries, more than fiction, may require an open political context to exist at all, and certainly require freedom to flourish.

ALGERIAN DOCUMENTARIES DURING THE CIVIL WAR

Algeria's Civil War can be described as two parallel (and to some extent successive) operations: first, the deployment of violence by the Islamists and the state, and second, a struggle over the public representation of that violence that has persisted long after the war ended. Following immediately on the cancellation of legislative elections in 1991, the Algerian regime began to employ—and to impose on other speakers through strict controls on national media—a discourse of "eradicationism," intended to dehumanize and criminalize the Islamist political opposition through the tropes of "terrorist" and "religious fanatic." We can here see the distribution of information, images, and descriptions as a state-controlled field where, according to journalist and activist Salima Ghezali, television, even more than print journalism or book publishing, became a real "*machine de guerre*" (war machine).[34]

---

[34] Quoted by Lahouari Addi in "L'armée algérienne confisque le pouvoir," *Le Monde Diplomatique*, February 1998.

In attempting to control the images and narrative of the Civil War, the state imposed censorship and organized propaganda campaigns, implemented primarily through the mass media. Access to basic information was severely limited throughout the 1990s. In September 1992, the regime declared that any act connected with "terrorism"—a category that the authorities expanded to include such supposed offenses as "frightening the population"—was punishable by imprisonment. The injunction specifically included "disseminating documents, images, or recordings" the state found offensive, as well as any attempt at "defending any act connected with 'acts of terrorism.'"[35] The Civil War predictably halted cinematographic production in Algeria. Few fiction films were produced, and even fewer directors were allowed to film on location, given the insecurity then reigning in Algeria. Documentaries were even more difficult to produce than before. Nevertheless, some Algerian filmmakers have tried to document what was happening in the country. Many of these had been living abroad for some time or had left the country for security reasons; they all felt the need to testify to the events of the early 1990s, and they naturally chose the documentary form. The documentaries produced by this international cohort were screened primarily on French TV channels like France Télévision or Arte.

Ahmed Lallem, who had left Algeria for France during the Civil War, felt compelled to find the women he had filmed in 1966 for his first documentary *Elles* (1967) and then directed *Algériennes 30 ans après* (1995), focusing on four of his original subjects who were living in exile and another four still in Algeria. Djamila Sahraoui, who had moved to France in 1975, directed a documentary called *La moitié du ciel d'Allah* (1995), featuring interviews with Algerian women about their work and their struggles for equality and freedom. In her later *Algérie, la vie quand même* (1998), she documents the daily life of Tazmalt, a village in the Kabylia region, seeking to counterbalance the images of massacres and killings that were emerging from Algeria during the Civil War. For *L'Algérie la vie toujours* (2001) Sahraoui asked her nephew and his friends to film themselves over the course of nine months. Filmmaker Malek Bensmaïl worked on several documentaries for French TV channels. The best known of

---

[35] Décret législatif no. 92-03 du 30 septembre 1992 relatif à la lutte contre la subversion et le terrorisme, 30 September 1992, chapter 1, Articles 1, 4, 5.

these is *Algérie (s)* (2002), which he directed with Thierry Leclère.[36] The film traces the history of the country from independence to the 1990s Civil War, attempting to trace the origins of the Civil War's violence; *Algérie (s)* chronicles the country's struggle for peace, stability, and democracy by combining recent and archival interviews, newsreel footage, and contemporary filmed footage from Algeria. (I will return to Bensmaïl's work in Chap. 1.)

Tariq Teguia was one of the few filmmakers to take on the task of producing independent films in Algeria during the tumultuous and dangerous period from 1993 to 2000. He began his cinematic career with four short movies shot during the Civil War: *Kech Movement* (1992), *Le Chien* (1996), *Ferrailes d'attente* (1998), and *La clôture* (2002). Some of the titles read as manifestos for a whole generation of directors. *Kech mouvement?* ("Is there any movement?") asks (in Algerian Arabic) what changes are happening within the country and within Algerian cinema. Teguia's films cover themes that become crucial for the new Algerian cinema as he tries to understand the nation's recent past rather than glorify past events in nationalistic terms. He examines restrictions on movement that constrain most Algerian citizens in their lives and considers a shared sense of being imprisoned or marginalized. His first feature film *Rome plutôt que vous* (2006), released a few years after the end of the Civil War, is, in its realism, aesthetically proximate to the documentary. Filming with a moving—even shaking—camera, Teguia follows his two main characters as they search for counterfeit passports and visas, portraying with a rare precision and humanity their hopes to leave Algeria for Europe. He films marginal characters with the obvious aim of reshaping the old nationalistic narrative of a unified nation—as this post-independence story had promptly been revived at the close of the Civil War. Teguia's choices of independent tone and low-cost techniques—he proved it was possible to make a movie on a tiny budget and outside the traditional systems of production—have encouraged many young filmmakers in the new generation that succeeded him after the beginning of the 2000s.

---

[36] The film is available on DVD. Thierry Leclère, Malek Bensmaïl and Patrick Barrat, *Algérie (s)*, Editions Montparnasse, 2004.

DOCUMENTARIES AFTER THE CIVIL WAR

After the horrors of the Civil War came to an end around 2000, Algerian filmmakers made a collective turn to reality. We see in the decade that followed a need to understand and to gather testimony. The filmmakers of this period—who had come of age during the Civil War—resolutely maintain their distance from the authoritative tone of the national media and state-funded movies, and they have also rejected global corporate media stereotypes—the endlessly repeated messaging around the notion of a timelessly troubled and problematic Algeria. And many of these post-Civil War Algerian filmmakers have chosen to produce documentaries rather than fictional films. Malek Bensmaïl's *Aliénations* (2005) and Habiba Djahnine's *Lettre à ma soeur* (2006) are among the earliest documentaries to explore the consequences of the Civil War in different communities, evidencing this new investigative and testimonial determination. Other filmmakers followed, among them **Karim Loualiche with** *Chantier A* (2013); Lamine Ammar Khodja with *Bla Cinéma* (2015); Bahia Bencheikh El Fegoun, *Fragments de rêve* (2018); Meriem Bouakaz Achour, *Nar* (2019); Fayçal Hammoum, *Vote Off* (2017), Amine Hattou, *Janitou* (2019); Drifa Mezenner Mzener, *J'ai habité l'absence deux fois* (2011); Abdenour Zahzah, *L'Oued, l'oued* (2014); and Salem Brahimi, *Abdelkader* (2014).[37]

In addition to the new cohort of documentary-minded filmmakers working in the country, other filmmakers of Algerian descent but born and raised in France have also produced documentaries about Algeria: this group working both in and out of Algeria includes Dorothée Myriam Kellou with *A Mansourah, tu nous as séparés* (2019), Mohamed Ouzine with *Samir dans la poussière* (2015), and Lina Soualem with *Leur Algérie* (2020). In 2016, the Algerian-French artist and filmmaker Katia Kameli dedicated a three-part documentary *Le roman algérien* (2016) to exploring, questioning, and translating what she calls the official national narrative. Silvia Mascheroni has analyzed the documentaries of Algerian and French Algerian women as examples of counter-narration in the contemporary Algerian and French public spheres,[38] opening the way for scholars who wish to work on Algerian and diasporic documentaries.

---

[37] I include here the documentary works of several filmmakers to whom I have not been able to dedicate individual chapters.

[38] Silvia Mascheroni, *Memorie. Donne e documentari nell'Algeria indipendente*, Libraccio Editore, 2021.

Considering the significant obstacles precluding the flourishing of an Algerian cinema, the sheer number of documentaries produced since 2000 (compared to the limited output in past decades) suggest that Algerian documentary as a genre has reached a crucial moment. The revival of documentaries in the 2000s has been driven by multiple factors. There is no doubt that the first democratic opening in Algeria in 1988, followed by the Civil War of the 1990s, challenged the processes of nationalist myth-making and contributed to the birth of this new cinematography. And this new filmmaking is, in turn, breaking with *cinéma moudjahid* and the national cinema of propaganda (still very much attached to the past) to engage directly with the present and its challenges.

The resurgence of the documentary genre is also undeniably related to technological innovations such as the digital camera, which makes filming easier and less expensive. Documentary film has always been a fluid form, and it is a form that has been reinvented over the years as filmmakers have taken advantage of successive generations of new media technology. Many directors interviewed for this book emphasized that even if the documentary form had always interested them—and many did recall an early fascination with documentaries—they could not deny that documentary film also simply represented a more realistic option than fiction, for both budgetary and technical reasons. As state funds became scarce, independent filmmakers began to adopt a more international and supranational mode of film production. These filmmakers have grown increasingly dissatisfied with the "national" paradigm of production, circulation, and consumption of their films; an increasingly interconnected, multicultural, and polycentric world has allowed them to seek funds from different sources and to find innovative ways of financing their films.[39] Many of the new documentary makers avoid the traditional financing circuits for Algerian films— which would restrict them to Algerian and French funding sources—instead seeking money from countries like Qatar, Belgium, Lebanon, the

---

[39] Numerous works have analyzed the supranational reach of North African cinema: Michael Gott and Thibaut Schilt, *Cinéma-Monde. Decentred Perspectives on Global Filmmaking in French*, Edinburgh University Press, 2018; Will Higbee and Song Hwee Lim, "Concepts of transnational cinema: towards a critical transnationalism in film studies", *Transnational Cinemas 1: 1*, pp. 7–21, 2018; Patricia Caillé, "Cinemas of the Maghreb': Reflections on the transnational and polycentric dimensions of regional cinema", *Studies in French Cinema* 13: 3, 2018, pp. 241–256. Abdelfettah Benchenna, Patricia Caillé and Nolwenn Mignant (dir.), *La circulation des films: Afrique du Nord et Moyen Orient. Africultures* n°101 -102, L'Harmattan, 2016.

Netherlands, and Switzerland. Producer and filmmaker Narimane Mari has also played an important role in promoting the works of young filmmakers in Algeria: she created her own production company, *Centrale Electrique*, to express her commitment to allowing young filmmakers to craft their cinematographic universes without worrying about state expectations.[40] The new filmmakers can then hope that their films will reach beyond their indigenous sites of production and beyond the handful of European film festivals that have dominated the international film circuit. Competing festivals now allow these new Algerian filmmakers to see their documentaries screened in the Arab world and in the world beyond. *143, rue du desert*, Hassen Ferhani's most recent documentary, was screened first at the Locarno Film Festival in August 2019, where Ferhani won the award for best emerging director, and the movie was later selected for the El Gouna Film Festival in Egypt, the Toronto International Film Festival, the *Festival International du Cinéma d'Alger* in Algiers, and then for *Les Rencontres Internationales du documentaire* in Montreal (to name only a few). These films also circulate through other informal channels, including screenings at universities and liberal arts colleges, especially in the U.S.

Technological innovations and shifts in modes of production and circulation have coincided with independent initiatives promoting the documentary form. Between 2007 and 2012, the *Association Cinéma Mémoire*, created by Habiba Djahnine, used the platform of the independent Béjaïa Film Festival—first established in 2003—to organize "Béjaïa docs," an annual program of documentary-making workshops. The program's stated objective was to train young Algerians in the use of audiovisual tools, as part of a broader educational project, involving both cinema professionals and socio-cultural counselors, to create and maintain a film training center. "Béjaïa docs" was a partnership between the Algerian *Cinéma mémoire* and *Kaina Cinéma*, a Paris-based association that promotes cultural exchanges between Algeria and other countries in the Mediterranean region, and *Les Ateliers Varan*, a Paris based nonprofit association that work, since 1980, to diversify forms of expression and communication through images. "Béjaïa Doc" followed the philosophy of *Les Ateliers Varan* to promote the ongoing use of direct and

---

[40] Narimane Mari began her career as a producer in 2001. In 2006 she became a founding member of *Centrale Electrique* and has continued producing as part of that company. *Central Electrique* has produced both of Ferhani's feature films and Djamel Kerkar's *Atlal* (2017). She also directed *Loubia Hamra* (2013) and *Le Fort des fous* (2017).

anthropologically inspired cinema. The films produced under its auspices were to exhibit a critical link to reality, using choices in film direction to question how reality might be represented. Each young filmmaker would be asked to choose for their documentary an environment close to their lived experience, either family or community. The initiative encouraged an entire generation of filmmakers to work in the documentary form: many promising young Algerian directors got their start with Béjaïa Doc. As a Béjaïa Doc participant in 2011, Drifa Mezner directed *J'ai habité l'absence deux fois*, a short film exploring her family's effort to come to terms with her brother's departure for England; she is now finishing a first documentary feature about celibacy among women in their late 30s. Bahia Bencheikh El Fegoun created a short documentary *C'est à Constantine* in 2008, following a woman through the city of Constantine, which the filmmaker had left when she was young; years later she directed *Fragments de rêves* (2017), which documents the rise of dissent in Algeria since 2011.

Habiba Djahnine has played a crucial role in the development of the documentary genre in Algeria. Poetry was Djahnine's first mode of creative expression. Before she began filming Algeria—documenting the nation's civil society and its activists—she published a book of poems titled *Outre-Mort* (Beyond death); the 2003 collection was a first artistic homage to her sister Nabila Djahnine, who was assassinated by Islamists during the Civil War, on February 15, 1995. Nabila Djahnine was a well-known feminist activist, president of the organization *Thighri N'tmettouth*, which means "women in protest" in Tamazight. After receiving multiple death threats, she was killed in front of her house. In a 2019 interview in Tunis, Habiba Djahnine explained to me that she left Algeria for France not long after her sister's death as she no longer felt safe, and she needed to mourn her sister's death. She learned the craft of filmmaking and then, after years in France, she decided to use the documentary form to revisit her sister's assassination and its impact on her and her immediate family: in 2005, she began shooting what would become her first documentary, *Lettre à ma soeur* (2006). The film addresses the personal and family-scale consequences of the assassination and analyses more broadly the consequences of political violence for Algerian society. Djahnine refutes the notion that violence is a characteristic intrinsic to Algerian society—as violence was often then characterized by the Algerian state and by national and Western media. Her other documentaries, *Autrement citoyens* (2008), *Retour à la montagne* (2010), and *Avant de franchir la ligne d'horizon* (2011), examine the details of activism and question preconceived narratives about feminism and political engagement: she shows her audiences the complexity of Algerian society and the reshaping of political engagement through the years.

Djahnine is still very much involved in forming filmmakers, through les *Ateliers de Création de Films Documentaires* in Timimoun, where she now lives. Each year Djahnine organizes workshops on documentary making through the *Ateliers*, including a 2018–2019 workshop that invited six young women filmmakers: Sonia At Qasi Kessi, Wiame Awres, Saadia Gacem, Kamila Ould Larbi, Leïla Saadna, and Kahina Zina. She is also involved in an effort to archive and make available to audiences and to scholars all the films produced during the years of *Atelier* workshops. In 2019, she started creating the platform *Imagine*, which will offer access to dozens of documentaries produced since 2007 in the workshops as well as masterclasses with filmmakers from Algeria and elsewhere. The *Imagine* site will be a goldmine for researchers who want to explore Algerian cultural productions—or to deconstruct the myth that cinema production in the country has been paralyzed since the Civil War. Attention can be paid for example to women filmmakers who take different venues than the immersive cinema that is at the core of this book.

For decades Algerian documentary production occupied a marginal position in a national cinema that favored fiction over nonfiction films. Even today, Algerian documentary is still arguably a marginalized category in an already marginal independent cinema. Algerian audiences rarely find opportunities to view independent documentaries outside special screenings during festivals or those organized by cinema clubs or, in the larger cities of Oran, Algiers, and Constantine, at the French Cultural Institute. These films never benefit from national release or distribution. But despite all the obstacles and difficulties, they do exist. They give agency to the directors and to the subjects filmed and to the critics and academics who wish to analyze their content. To measure their impact only by their circulation would be to underestimate how important they are in the larger process of democratizing the country.

References

Arasoughly, Alia (dir.). *Screens of life. Critical Film Writing from the Arab World.* Quebec: World Heritage Press, 1996.

Bedjaoui, Ahmed. *Cinéma et guerre de libération. Algérie, des batailles d'images.* Algiers : Chihab, 2014.

Benchenna, Abdelfettah and Patricia Caillé and Nolwenn Mignant (dir.). *La circulation des films: Afrique du Nord et Moyen Orient*. Paris: L'Harmattan, 2016.

Berrah, Mouny and Bachy, Victor and Ben Salma, Mohand and Boughedir Férid, CinémAction (dir). *Cinémas du Maghreb*. Revue trimestrielle- N 14, Spring 1981.

Boudjedra, Rachid. *Naissance du cinéma algérien*. Paris : Éditions François Maspéro, 1971.

Bruzzi, Stella. *New Documentary, Second Ed.* London and New York: Routledge, 2006.

Caillé, Patricia. « On the Shifting Significance of 'Algerian Cinema' as a Category of Analysis, in Rabah Aissaoui and Claire Eldridge (ed.), *Algeria revisited: history, culture and iden*tity. London, New York: Bloomsbury Academic, 2017.

Caillé, Patricia. "Cinemas of the Maghreb': Reflections on the transnational and polycentric dimensions of regional cinema", *Studies in French Cinema* 13: 3, 2018: 241-256.

Dadci, Younès. *Dialogues Algérie-cinéma : première histoire du cinéma algérien*. Algiers : Éditions Dadci, 1970.

Denis, Sébastien. *Le Cinéma et la guerre d'Algérie : la propagande à l'écran (1945-1962)*. Paris: Nouveau Monde éditions, 2009.

Djahnine, Habiba. "Des regards libres du cinéma algérien. Uncovered Eyes of Algerian Cinema. A conversation on *La Zerda* et les Chants de l'oubli and *Monangambeee*, in *Specters of Freedom. Cinema and Decolonization*, [DVD booklet]Arsenal, 2018.

Forgacs, David. "Italians in Algiers", *Interventions*. - Vol. 9, n. 3, 2007: 350-364.

Gott, Michael and Thibaut Schilt. *Cinéma-Monde. Decentered Perspectives on Global Filmmaking in French*. Edinburgh: Edinburgh University Press, 2018

Higbee, Will and Song Hwee Lim, "Concepts of transnational cinema: towards a critical transnationalism in film studies", *Transnational Cinemas 1: 1* (2018): 7-21.

Layerle, Sébastien. « Premières images de l'Algérie indépendante : *Un peuple en marche* (1964) ou « l'épopée » du Centre audiovisuel d'Alger », *Décadrages* [On line], 2016 : 29-30.

Megherbi, Abdelghani. *Le miroir apprivoisé*. Alger : ENAL, 1985.

Megherbi, Abdelghani. *Le miroir aux alouettes*. Alger : ENAL, 1985.

Meherzi, Lotfi. *Le cinéma algérien : institutions, imaginaire, idéologie*. Algiers: SNED, 1980.

Salmane, Hala and Simon Hartog and David Wilson, *Algerian Cinema*. London; British Film Institute, 1976.

Stora, Benjamin. « Le cinéma algérien entre deux guerres », *Confluences Méditerranée*, No. 81 (Feb. 2012) : 181-188

Tamzali, Wassyla. *En attendant Omar Gatlato*. Algiers: ENAP, 1979.

Van de Peer, Stefanie. *Negotiating Dissidence. The Pioneering Women of Arab Documentary*. Edinburgh: Edinburgh University Press, 2017.

CHAPTER 3

Malek Bensmaïl: The Legacy of the Revolution and the Question of Democracy

"Where to find strength, in order to live according to honor?"
—Alexander Sokurov

Resister c'est aussi penser le regard ("To resist is also to think about how you see things"). We can read this challenging sentence on the home page of Malek Bensmaïl's official website. From the beginning of his career, Bensmaïl has considered the documentary an act of resistance: in film after film, he has built a career in which showing means resisting. For Malek Bensmaïl, cinema is an act of resistance against authoritarianism and the non-democratic system that has existed in Algeria since 1962. Algerians have seen, on the one hand, what has become of the *Front de libération nationale* party (FLN) after 1962 that systematically constructed a mythological representation of the past that would justify its own power, and, on the other hand, successive regimes which have repeatedly hindered their access to democracy and freedom. Against this fictional construct of the past and the reality of present obstacles, documentary making becomes a way to resist, offering spectators a view onto the structural barriers that exist in their own society and also questioning the official memories that frame and sustain the present. In considering the documentary a "barometer for democracy" (as we have seen in Chap. 2), Bensmaïl has emphasized the documentary's capacity to "show our reality." Rather than stopping at the question of whether film has the capacity to represent

M. Belkaïd, *From Outlaw to Rebel*, Palgrave Studies in Arab Cinema, https://doi.org/10.1007/978-3-031-19157-2_3

reality, he asks further how Algeria can move toward democracy if film-makers' efforts to engage with the reality around them are censored or denied distribution.

With more than 15 television documentaries and 6 creative documentaries produced since 1996, Malek Bensmaïl has, with Habiba Djahnine, led the way to a revival of the documentary genre in Algerian cinema. Hassen Ferhani and Djamel Kerkar, considered in Chaps. 4 and 5, stress their debt to Bensmaïl and his work. And returning to the conversation with Ferhani and Kerkar that opened Chap. 2, Bensmaïl has offered his own explanation for the dominance of fiction in Algerian film since 1962. During my interview with him in April 2021, Bensmaïl emphasized the particular work that documentaries do compared to fiction, and how that work is in tension with the goals of an authoritarian government:

> With fiction we can bypass censorship. Metaphors and allegories help do that. The documentary has a more frontal approach to reality; it allows us to see ourselves. Algerian-type regimes don't like to see themselves on screen. Documentaries reflect everything that does not work in the country: mis-management, corruption, incompetence, and bad governance. For fiction we can always say that it is a reinterpretation of reality. This argument doesn't work so well with documentaries.[1]

Bensmaïl himself divides his films into two groups: the first corresponds to his cinematic inclination and what he calls immersive and sometimes "wisemanian" films, in reference to filmmaker Frederick Wiseman's immersive approach to documentary-making. The second group includes more didactic and historical films; it is necessary, even urgent, to make these films before all witnesses of those past events disappear. In the latter category is the most recent documentary he produced for the French and German channel Arte, *Toute l'Algérie du Monde* (2021), on Algerian diplomacy during Bouteflika's presidency. Others include *Boudiaf un espoir assassiné* (1999); *Algérie(s)* (2002) (mentioned in Chap. 1); *Guerres secrètes du FLN en France* (2012); and to some extent *La Bataille d'Alger. Un film dans l'histoire* (2017), in which he explores the making and the afterlife of the iconic political film *La Bataille d'Alger* (1965). Bensmaïl summarizes his work in these terms:

---

[1] Interview realized in September 2021. All subsequent quotes from Bensmaïl will be from this interview.

Some films like *Aliénations*, *La Chine*, etc. correspond more to my inclination, my desire for cinema. They need time to be created and allow me to express my own sensibilities. The other films are more urgent, less aesthetic, they might not correspond to my favorite form of filmmaking, but they are • necessary for our country (Algeria) as they record testimony that needs to be shared. We are not attentive enough to discourses and testimonies, and actors of the past might die without having been able to share their experience with us.

Following Bensmaïl's own nomenclature, this chapter focuses on three immersive documentaries: *Aliénations* (2004), *La Chine est encore loin* (2008), and *Contre-pouvoirs* (2016). *Aliénations* (2004) documents the daily life of doctors and patients in the psychiatric hospital of Constantine, where Bensmaïl's father worked. *La Chine est encore loin* (2008) studies the collective memory of the Algerian Revolution in Ghassira, a small village in the Aurès, one of the regions where the revolution began in 1954. *Contre-pouvoirs* (2016) follows the journalists of *El Watan*, one of the most important francophone newspapers in the country.

Bensmaïl mentions the influence of Russian filmmaker Alexandre Sokurov, with whom he had extended conversations about filmmaking during 1988, a year Bensmaïl spent studying cinema in Russia. Bensmaïl has a deep admiration for Sokurov's work: "Alexander Sokurov opened my eyes to documentary. His films are extremely sensitive, and immersive too, but harsher and deeper than Weisman's films, which revolve mainly around institutions. Sokurov is able to capture the depths of the human condition in a very challenging and difficult political context." Bensmaïl recognizes that in his immersive films he is also, on many levels, faithful to the *direct cinema* tradition and Wiseman's approach to filming, where the director engages in minimal intervention while filming. Bensmaïl often captures his characters in what appear to be natural situations, through non-mediated real-time sequences, and he works diligently to convey the ambient sounds of the sites he is filming. He nevertheless departs from Wiseman's approach when he also takes the liberty of intervening in the situations he is filming to ask direct questions to his characters. And in *Aliénations* (though not in his other immersive films), he takes the further step of implementing a voice-over or commentary voice, explaining directly to the audience how much the film owes to his father, who worked at the hospital he is filming, thus revealing his personal involvement with the topic. Most importantly, he insists that he makes his films *with* the subjects he films and not *about* them. And he establishes what he calls a "democratic relationship" with the characters which he understands in the sense of a collaborative and consensual effort:

> I make films with people. Films about people is what television does in Algeria but also in France and the United States. Making films with people means making and taking the time to explain and spending long periods not filming. For *Aliénations*, I took the time to explain why I wanted to film a psychiatric hospital. Algeria was talking about the deaths of the martyrs and not enough about the living. It is also out of the question for me to entrap my characters ... to trap a character in his own error. The documentary must give everyone, even a negative character; the opportunity to get out of it. So I regularly show the rushes—every two days or so—so that people can see themselves and make an informed decision to continue being filmed or not.

In the end, Bensmaïl delivers what appears to be a transparent experience of the settings and the voices he films. And yet on further inspection we see significant mediations through three interrelated devices: editing, transition shots, and elements of contextualization. Each of the films analyzed in this chapter has a sequential organization in which different characters are filmed in the same place. The sequencing, the transition shots, and the elements of contextualization allow the director to produce a global and intelligible narrative that suggests the Algerian social predicament is reflected in the film's characters. I see the immersive and observational documentaries directed by Bensmaïl as a synecdoche: the filmed microcosms are made to represent Algerian society in its entirety, the filmed characters' individual sufferings and challenges serving as the outcome and the reflection of Algeria's political and social crisis. The films are in clear opposition to the triumphalist discourse developed by the FLN and the Algerian state in the years since independence. These works, like others analyzed in this book, contribute to building an alternative version of the past and a better and more nuanced understanding of the present. The spectator is invited to hear different stories, from schoolteachers to pupils, to explore different places from Constantine in *Aliénations* to Ghassira in *La Chine est encore loin,* and to witness diverse political and social positions and trajectories: these counterbalance the distorted representations of some films of *cinéma moudjahid*, imposed by the bureaucratic state and the successive regimes. Bensmaïl uses a technique and aesthetic of immersion to question the Algerian regime's nationalist and official discourse on two levels. The first level is focused on interrogating the revolution's legacy in contemporary Algeria (*La Chine est encore loin*). The second level is focused instead on exploring the challenges Algeria has faced since the brief democratic opening of 1988 and the 1990s Civil War that followed (*Aliénations, Contre-pouvoirs*).

THE LEGACY OF THE REVOLUTION

La Chine est encore loin (2008) is an important shift in Bensmaïl's career: all the films he directed prior to this documentary were filmed in Algeria and funded by the French *Centre National du Cinéma* (CNC) or by French public or European television channels. For this new film, Bensmaïl sought funds from the Algerian Ministry of Culture. When he had used only half the amount authorized, Algerian television (ENTV) reviewed an early edited draft version of the film and denied access to the remaining funds—because Bensmaïl says, the film had "challenged the official state history." Bensmaïl then used French and other funds to finish the film. Nicole Beth Wallenbrock, writing about representations of the "Franco-Algerian war," has articulated an argument that *La Chine est encore loin* (2008) is "ostensibly for French eyes" and that "a degree of visual colonization continues" as a result of the film's financing and, to some extent, because of the ways it represents the Algerian reality.[2] This chapter responds to that argument by re-viewing the film through an Algerian lens that doesn't always imply an anticolonial intent but rather an exploration of Algerian memory. I will consider first the relationship between financing and audience: the scarcity of public and private funding in Algeria explains why Bensmaïl (like many other filmmakers discussed in this book) was forced to rely on French funds. That funding is obtained from France—or, for that matter, from any other foreign source, whether European or Arab—is not sufficient evidence to conclude that the resulting film is made exclusively or primarily for a French or foreign audience.[3] More importantly, rather than see traces of visual colonization in Bensmaïl's work, I insist that *La Chine est encore loin* instead demonstrates the

[2] Nicole Beth Wallenbrock, *The Franco-Algerian War through a Twenty-first Century Lens. Film and History. Bloomsbury*, 2020, p. 48.

[3] Even if he has benefitted from French funds, Bensmaïl has reiterated in our interview in April 2021, his primary goal to reach an Algerian audience, despite the structural problems of Algerian cinema. In pursuit of his Algerian audience, he even went so far as to facilitate the circulation of pirated DVDs of *La Chine est encore loin*.

filmmaker's ability to challenge long-standing myths about Algeria and the Algerian War of Independence and thus to oppose a falsified and incomplete version of the past—a state-constructed narrative that prevents Algeria from achieving complete freedom and from "deciphering the present and imagining the future," to use the words of Algerian historian Mohammed Harbi.[4] Bensmaïl's is a critical and decolonial gaze: to suggest that he reproduces (whether consciously or not) a colonial perspective can lead us to a critical impasse in which any filmmaker who seeks French funds and then films Algerian realities through a critical lens would be suspected of "a colonial downward gaze at the Other."[5] Bensmaïl rather invokes a decolonized gaze: without ever insulting the legacy of the revolution, he allows himself to question the official version that focuses mainly on the accomplishments and triumphs of the FLN rather than giving a more nuanced and humanized narrative of what happened before and during the war, within the FLN and the nationalist movement.

The film starts by offering the spectator some contextual details about the site at the center of the documentary's narrative: "On November 1, 1954, a French teacher, his wife, and an Algerian governor were victims of an attack near the Berber village of Ghassira. This act signaled the start of Algeria's war for independence and turned the Aurès into the cradle of the revolution." Two hours and ten minutes later, the documentary ends with a hadith of the Prophet Mohammed, a key to the film's title and purpose. "La Chine est encore loin" or "China is still far away" refers to the obligation to "seek knowledge, even as far away as China." As China, in the film's title, remains at a distance, so too does the understanding of the War of Independence. Between these elements inserted at the opening and closing of the film, Bensmaïl hopes to tell a story of the deterioration of memory—in other words, of knowledge—in the village he films over 50 years after the war began there. Bensmaïl's original project was to film a classroom in Algeria; he wanted to examine the educational system, with a focus on its challenges and shortcomings. He had already worked in his hometown Constantine for his documentary *Aliénations,* so he had decided against filming his childhood elementary school. During his research for the new film, he discovered the story of the French teacher who died in November 1954, during one of the first FLN-led attacks; he chose then to set his film in the school in the village near which the War of Independence started.

---

[4] Mohammed Harbi, *La Guerre commence en Algérie.* Editions Complexe, 1984, p. 5.
[5] Nicole Beth Wallenbrock, *The Franco-Algerian War,* p. 48.

It is clear from the start that Bensmaïl chose the village of Ghassira for its historical significance, even though, as Denise Brahimi has mentioned, the village is situated in what was also formerly a popular tourist region.[6] To an uninformed eye, the contextualization would point to the complexity of the events that occurred in the village in 1954, specifically mentioning the two French civilian victims of the November 1 attack: the French teacher Guy Monnerot and his wife Jacqueline. Official communications from the FLN announcing their actions on November 1 specifically mentioned that no civilians were to be targeted. As for the attack near Ghassira, Harbi has described an FLN commando team led by Bachir Chihani organizing an ambush on the Tighanimine road. The FLN force stopped a bus transporting travelers—including the Algerian governor (Caïd) of M'chounèche, Hadj Sadok, and the Monnerots, a married French couple who worked as teachers at Ghassira's elementary school. The governor showed open disdain for the attackers and ultimately reached for his weapon. Sbaïhi, one of the men of the commando group, started shooting. Guy Monerot was killed and his wife wounded.[7]

If the spectator already knows the events, they will notice that Bensmaïl completes the contextualization with several transitional shots—situated throughout the film—that point both to the events of 1954 and to Ghassira's importance as a site in the collective memory. Throughout the film the viewer can see a bus going through the mountains and the village streets that the director intentionally figures as significant and a clear reference to the attack. Bensmaïl also films, for just a few seconds, a bus that has been drawn on a classroom blackboard. During this transitional scene, someone throws pieces of chalk at the blackboard; when they strike the board, they sound like rifle shots. The Algerian flag is also omnipresent, as is the national anthem, sung by students at the raising of the flag each week. The imbrication of images and sounds links scenes as an echo of past events and of a central sequence in which Bensmaïl films the official celebration of November 1, in Ghassira.

In this celebration scene, Bensmaïl's camera captures a heated exchange between several men. The celebrations, as solemn as they appear to be (grandiose speeches, military music), are far from univocal. The problem seems to revolve around the official list of the men who will be mentioned

---

[6] Denise Brahimi, « La Chine est encore loin. Un film de Malek Bensmaïl (2008) », in *Regards sur les cinémas du Maghreb*. Editions Petra, Paris, 2016, p. 201.

[7] Mohammed Harbi, *La Guerre commence*, pp. 21–22.

as combatants or *moudjahidin* who participated in the bus attack near Ghassira. The villagers insist that the list of heroes is incomplete, and they ask for official documentation to back it up. One of the men, Ammar Ben Mohamed Laggoune, proudly states, "I am the official document," and then continues counting out names, and concluding, "We were seven. Whoever says the contrary is lying."

In the following scene, Bensmaïl films a man behind a fence: he is attending the celebrations, but he remains outside the official space of commemoration. He looks into Bensmaïl's camera and says that he was a member of the commando team that led the attack on the bus: "I can talk about it, but not here, I have all the papers." The man's revelation—and the suggestion that he could only speak of his participation far away from the official events (and probably the authorities)—casts a shadow on the official speech the viewer can hear going on in the background: "Dear brothers, this region can lay claim to the honor of having launched the armed revolution under the command of the hero Mostefa Ben Boulaid and his companions."

Mostefa Ben Boulaid was indeed chief of the region, and he did die during the Algerian War of Independence. Mentioning his name is important. And yet centering the story on this departed hero confirms a tendency of what historian Hassen Remaoun calls an "anonymous narrative[8]"—a narrative that centers and celebrates the names of the dead while survivors bargain with the official authorities to include their names, and may be both symbolically and actually excluded from the commemorative events. The man Bensmaïl films, whose name does not appear on the official list and who is quite literally forced to the margins of the official celebration, is one of them. Bensmaïl explained during our interview that his name is Djaghrouri; he is one of the men who mistakenly shot the Monnerots, while aiming for Hadj Sadok. To understand his excommunication from the formal commemoration is to understand that the events as they actually transpired do not serve the narrative of a heroic FLN, nor of November 1 as the founding moment of the national struggle. In other words, a national origin story that centers on the accidental shooting of two civilians is not heroic, and so the men who actually pulled their

---

[8] See Hassen Remaoun, « L'enseignement de l'Histoire de la Guerre de libération nationale à travers une lecture des manuels scolaires algériens », *Internationale Schulbuchforschung, Algerien, Frankreich und der Algerienkrieg, France and the Algerian War*, 2004, vol.26 No. 1, pp. 59–74.

triggers on November 1, 1954 are anonymized as "companions"—and the story of civilian casualties goes untold.

It took a number of weeks for Bensmaïl to establish a relationship of trust with Djaghrouri and to convince him to tell his story before it was too late (Bensmaïl confirms that the man has died in the years since the film was made). Djaghrouri specifically asked to be filmed in the cemetery where his brothers in arms were buried. In telling his own story, he has the opportunity to explain that he aimed to shoot Hadj Sadok, but in the course of firing 36 bullets, he was not able to avoid the Monnerots (Fig. 3.1). In Djaghrouri's telling, the death of Guy Monnerot was a mistake. This version was corroborated in 1954 when the FLN monthly political bulletin described the civilian deaths as "unpremeditated."[9] That 50 years later the man who allegedly fired the first shots in the war of independence is excluded from the celebration of the date he raised his gun, leads the viewer to reconsider the nature of the story presented as "official." We see the death of Guy Monnerot used to build a narrative that

Fig. 3.1 Djaghrouri, one of the men who mistakenly shot Guy Monnerot and his wife during the attack of November 1, 1954, telling his story in *La Chine est encore loin*

[9] Mohammed Harbi, Gilles Meynier, *Le FLN: Documents et histoire (1954-1962)*. Fayard, 2004, p. 32.

could humanize the members of the FLN and their actions. The shooter is indeed an ordinary man not fully trained as a soldier and he made mistakes that, in the circumstances of that roadside attack, were probably inevitable. But the FLN, as Mohamed Harbi has shown, has instead opted for a glorified version of the past in which the attacks of November 1954 have been retold as a founding and flawless moment.

> Reference or alibi, November 1954 has produced representations that tend to substitute legend for true history. Paradoxically, it is through this account that Algerians affirm their entry into the assembly of nations. As elsewhere, the cult of the dead, the hero-martyrs and brilliant actions conceal, for the sake of the Prince's conscience, the tensions and sufferings of the living.

> *Référence ou alibi, Novembre 1954 a suscité des représentations qui tendent à substituer la légende à l'histoire réelle. Paradoxalement, c'est par ce biais que les Algériens affirment leur entrée dans le concert des nations. Comme ailleurs, le culte des morts, des héros-martyrs et des actions d'éclat dissimulent, pour la bonne conscience du Prince, les tensions et les souffrances des vivants.*[10]

Harbi stresses the mythical aspect of November 1 and how this date has been instrumentalized to shape a narrative that served the FLN's political purposes after independence:

> According to a long-held myth, November 1954 emerged, fully armed, from the heads of the FLN founders. In fact, these men, trying to get the national movement out of a dead end, have appropriated for themselves the Algerians' long history of struggle.

> *Selon un mythe longtemps répandu, Novembre 1954 est sorti, armé de pied en cap, du cerveau des fondateurs du FLN. En fait ceux-ci, en sortant le mouvement national de l'impasse, se sont approprié le long passé de lutte des Algériens.*[11]

Instead of featuring a triumphal sequence, the events as they happened in Ghassira should help situate the FLN within a larger narrative that explains the steps that led to its creation and acknowledges that in 1954 the FLN was not yet as well organized as it would become in the years that

---

[10] Mohammed Harbi, *La Guerre commence,* p. 8.
[11] Mohammed Harbi, *La Guerre commence,* p. 6.

followed. The men belonging to the commando force were brave and patriotic, but they were not fully trained. Excluding Djaghrouri from the official list of participants and from the anniversary celebrations is an overt falsification. A commemorative project that begins from this truncated version of facts seems to lead directly to the process of memory deterioration that Bensmaïl examines in the rest of the documentary.

The film's sequential organization allows the viewer to follow different characters to different locations, but it seems that all roads lead to the village's school. It is there that the deterioration of memory is the most visible. That is the destination the bus seems to be approaching at the beginning of the film, as the viewer later recognizes the two schoolteachers among its passengers. The film ends with another bus, this time carrying students on a field trip to the beach. The numerous buses in the film's transitional sequences allow Bensmïl to juxtapose the past with the present.

Moreover, in an extended scene, Bensmaïl places his camera in one of the classrooms. He uses an omniscient lens to invite the viewer into the learning environment. The viewer can observe everything that happens in the classroom, even the students' whispers that the teacher is not supposed to hear. The audience follows several young pupils during their classes in French, math, and of course history.

In one evocative scene, which I mentioned in opening to this book, the students at the elementary school are not quite able to identify which country colonized Algeria. In addition to France, they offer answers as improbable as Mauritania, Spain, Australia, Brazil, and the United States. When asked about their families' relationship to the war of independence, one student has to admit that none of his relatives fought. Bensmaïl's microphone then catches the student whispering irreverent remarks about the teacher, then adding a few seconds later, "Damn your *moudjahidin*." When Bensmaïl films the young students' relative ignorance of the Algerian War, he shows that the distance between the students and the revolutionary legacy is less chronological than experiential—a distinction that Wallenbrock mentions—but he does not, as Wallenbrock further argues, "frame this ignorance for a (primarily) French audience."[12] He instead questions whether the Algerian educational system is capable of teaching the past effectively.

The Algerian War of Independence has always had a special place in lessons on Algerian history, beginning as early as elementary school. In 2000

---

[12] Nicole Beth Wallenbrock, *The Franco-Algerian War*, p. 48.

a national commission (*Commission Nationale de Réforme du Système Educatif* (CNRSE)) worked on proposals to reform the Algerian school system and its educational curriculum and in 2002, a new guide on teaching history was implemented at the high school, middle school, and elementary school levels. Students in their third year of elementary school (rather than the fifth year, as previously) were to be introduced to the history and origins of "the Great revolution of Liberation."[13] The old curricula, as analyzed by Hassan Remaoun, taught mainly a "heroic and anonymous" past in which only those who died as martyrs were named. The new textbooks relativize, to some extent, some of the tenacious myths perpetuated by the FLN, by mentioning for example other important figures of the nationalist movement like Messali Hadj and Ferhat Abbas.[14] But many of the old taboos remain and history is still told through the lens of a triumphant FLN. The history taught in schools thus echoes the official celebration of November 1—an event with which students have difficulty identifying. Bensmaïl implies the students' sense of distance from this celebrated past in a transitional scene where the camera films children watching the celebrations of November 1 from a distant hill, displaying little interest in what they see.

Paradoxically Ghassira, labeled "the cradle of the revolution" in the opening to *La Chine est encore loin*, is for now a place of forgetting—even though the witnesses and actors of past events are still alive and could share their memories and experiences with present-day students. The deterioration of memory is the overarching narrative that Bensmaïl tells in his documentary, but history can still be interrogated and saved from oblivion and from the deformations it has endured over time. Bensmaïl's documentary is an attempt to reinsert some memories and some truths into a half-forgotten and partly misshapen history of the war for independence: he does so by inviting characters of the past to speak to his modern audience and also by showing the freedom of today's children who remain unimpressed by the myths and legends taught in their classrooms or conveyed to them in other official communications. In her experimental film *Loubia Hamra* (2013), Narimane Mari takes a step further by asking

---

[13] Hassen Remaoun, « L'enseignement de l'Histoire de la Guerre », p. 6.

[14] One important shift in the new educational curriculum is that it addresses – albeit succinctly – the actions of parties other than the FLN that played a role in the nationalist movement, mainly the *Mouvement nationaliste Algérien* (MNA) of Messali Hadj and the *Union démocratique du manifeste algérien* (UDMA) founded by Ferhat Abbas.

children to reenact the Algerian War of Independence. In the film the children are told that Algerian soldiers only ate red beans, so their punishment for a "French soldier" they capture is to endure a diet exclusively composed of red beans. The children's playfulness is in both Mari's and Bensmaïl works a way to address myths and overcome wounds and traumas.

SOCIAL MALAISE AND THE QUESTION OF DEMOCRACY.

In the opening of *Contre-pouvoirs* (2015), Bensmaïl explains to his audience that he has "immersed" his camera within the headquarters of the newspaper *El Watan* in Algiers. He had made a similar choice of immersion in *Le Grand Jeu* (2005) when he followed Ali Benflis, then secretary general of the FLN party, during his presidential campaign against the president-candidate Abdelaziz Bouteflika. And in 2004, his camera had filmed the patients and medical team of a psychiatric hospital where the filmmaker's father had formerly worked. The cinematic choice of immersion is the common denominator among these films, and again in 2015 this choice allows Bensmaïl to tell multiple stories through his use of editing, transitional sequences, and contextualization. In his editing choices, the filmmaker works to build a coherent universe and an overarching narrative: all the men and women filmed are in some sense subject to political, economic, and social constraints, and they all face a reality over which they have little or no control.

Alienations, Imaginaries, and Trauma

Aliénations (2004) aims at understanding the suffering of patients in the psychiatric hospital of Constantine. The conscious and unconscious behaviors of the patients and the medical teams reveal the disintegration of a society undergoing significant political change and affected by tensions between tradition and modernity.[15] Baudouin Dupret has analyzed the film's sequencing to show how Bensmaïl "portrays the people's

---

[15] For an analysis of the tensions between modernity and tradition (including the background of popular culture) and on the film's presentation of psychiatry as one among many forms of mental care work, see Baudouin Dupret, *Practices of Truth: An ethnomethodological inquiry into Arab contexts*, John Benjamins Publishing Company, 2011.

alienation as the mirror of the country's alienation."[16] The film strives to grasp Algeria's broader social malaise through the words and attitudes of the hospital patients, exposing undercurrents that for some time have been feeding into an Algerian social crisis.

Filmed in 2003, four years after the official end of the Algerian Civil War, Bensmaïl's documentary emphasizes the psychological consequences of the war's tragic events. Algeria's Civil War officially ended when the parliament adopted the Civil Concord of 1999, which Abdelaziz Bouteflika implemented during his first term. The concord offered amnesty to Islamists who were willing to cease violent action: under its terms, members of armed groups who surrendered during the six months beginning July 13, 1999, and who had not killed, raped, or planted bombs in public places would be granted immunity from prosecution. Those who had committed the excluded crimes as part of their opposition to the state would receive reduced sentences, and they would benefit from further sentencing reductions if they surrendered to the authorities within three months. Bensmaïl, filming in the wards of the Constantine hospital four years later, communicates to the spectator that mental healing for Algerian society is far from complete; as the hospital patients express their fears, Bensmaïl's transitional shots reinforce the connections between the hospital and its patients and the broader Algerian society beyond its doors.

The political arena is the leitmotiv of the patients' discourse—from Bouteflika—whom a patient named Nawel mentions constantly in her rather long and incoherent tirades, to the FLN whose electoral results patients comment on during a visit to the barber. One responds to the FLN's (inevitable) victory in the most recent election with a rhetorical question: "Did they gain independence for nothing?" In a subsequent scene, the same patient joins another in singing the political slogans "tahya El Djazaier" ("long live Algeria") and "Yahya FLN" ("long live the FLN") while looking straight at Bensmaïl's camera. Their singing is clearly addressed to the filmmaker, and the patients smile mischievously as they sing, bringing us back to the predominant position the FLN occupies not only in the political arena but also in the popular imagination.

No other subject is mentioned as frequently as the Civil War and its aftermath. The topic of terrorism appears in several scenes, brought up by several different patients. One man, who seems to be going through a psychotic episode, keeps repeating that he is being harassed by the local authorities, who want him to be an informant. Over and over he insists, "I

---

[16] Baudouin Dupret, *Practices of Truth*, p. 135.

am not a terrorist," and he contrasts his precarious situation to the comfortable circumstances he imagines for the reformed terrorists amnestied by the 1999 Concord. He bitterly concludes: "The bush (*le maquis*) is rewarding" and "The state drove me crazy." When he is admitted to the hospital toward the end of the documentary, a transitional sequence shows two policemen waiting in the doorway. By this point, the spectator has had previous opportunities to notice a police wagon stationed near the hospital and the omnipresence of barred windows and closed rooms. Together these elements imply that the psychiatric hospital is explicitly bound to politics, the State, and the police.

Terrorism also comes up as Bensmaïl's camera witnesses a patient named Bouthobza and two other patients who are in a room, about to share a cigarette (Fig. 3.2). The tension is palpable, with Bouthobza asserting power over a cigarette that seems to belong to him. The conversation shifts to the aftermath of the Civil War and the question of peace:

> – *You know, when I'm home, I talk about nothing but peace. I want to talk to the terrorists and lead them towards peace. I want to bring peace to the world. I want to talk to the terrorists and the leaders of the whole world to make peace, because we are all brothers. Why are we killing each other? What's the point? Why are we killing each other? We are killing each other for... I want peace for the whole world. I want to talk to head-terrorist Merzag Madani, because he signed the civil agreement with the State. Why can't he go and see the GIA, who are killing people, and talk to them, with respect of course, and convince them?*
> – *But they don't want to understand.*
> – *They don't understand.*
> – *They don't understand diplomacy.*
> – *Has anyone tried?*
> – *I don't know.*
> – *I want to know if anyone has talked peace with the GIA? Why don't the authorities neutralize them?*
> – *If we weren't short of cigarettes and coffee, we'd be fine.*

In his emotional plea for peace, Bouthobza mentions Madani Merzag, formerly a national *emir* (commander) of the dissolved *Armée islamique du salut* (AIS). The AIS was founded in Algeria on July 18, 1994, as the "fighting wing" of the party *Front islamique du salut* (FIS); Mezrag was

Fig. 3.2 Patients of Constantine psychiatric hospital, sharing a cigarette and talking about war and peace in *Aliénations*

among the founders. As early as 1995, the AIS sought to negotiate a political solution with the regime; that early effort at reconciliation is why Bouthobza would now see him as a likely person to negotiate with the *Groupes islamiques armés* (GIA) (Armed Islamic Group). The GIA had emerged in 1993 to fight the regime—and anyone else they thought might be opposed to the Islamist movement. Among the many terrorist groups that took part in the Algerian Civil War, the GIA was the most radical and violent,[17] which is why Bouthabza's interlocutor doubts their willingness to join in diplomatic negotiations. During a simple conversation that starts and ends with a discussion of cigarettes, the tumultuous recent past is invited into the patient's room. Meanwhile the spectator hears not only a conversation about peace and politics but also, in the

---

[17] James Ciment, *Algeria: The Fundamentalist Challenge*. Facts on File, 1997.

background, a thunderstorm. The storm then becomes the topic of a series of transition shots, with dark clouds, in Dupret's words, "transporting the spectator out of the hospital, in the darkness and the tormented sky of the tempest."[18] The storm works here as a metaphor of a troubled outside world that continues to threaten the patients' peace of mind. The filmmaker's insistence on conveying ambient sounds, a technical device highly characteristic of the immersive approach, further uses the metaphor of the storm to bring the Algerian patients into participation in a wider storytelling.

Aliénations begins as a tribute to the filmmaker's father, by immersing itself in the hospital where he used to work. During the editing process, Bensmaïl chose to feature as characters what he calls "borderline" patients, ones who were not suffering from severe mental illness and thus could, in some sense, stand in for the filmmaker or the spectator. By exploring those patients' pains and anxieties the film ends up being an exploration of Algerian society and the demons that were haunting it. As early as 2003, it conveys the traumas of the Civil War that Djamel Kerkar will explore more fully in his 2016 documentary *Atlal* (Chap. 4).

The Media Between Hope and Paralysis

Bensmaïl filmed *Le Grand Jeu* in 2004, during the presidential campaign that led to President Bouteflika's second term in office. The film follows Bouteflika's challenger Ali Benflis from Algiers to Bouira, El Oued, Biskra, Aïn Touita, Tizi Ouzzou, and other cities. Ten years after the 2004 election, Abdelaziz Bouteflika is running for a fourth mandate. He has persuaded the national parliament to amend the constitution, removing the original two-term limit on the presidency. Ali Benflis is again one of Bouteflika's opponents, but during this new campaign the president is invisible. An illness has kept him out of the public eye since July 2013 and the official election campaign has started without him. Like its predecessor, the documentary Bensmaïl creates around this election is without suspense: the election results unsurprisingly favor Bouteflika with 81.53% of the votes, while 12.18% go to Ali Benflis.

If *Le Grand jeu* followed the 2004 campaign through the trajectory of Ali Benflis, this time Bensmaïl—with the help of Hassen Ferhani (chapter 4) as first assistant—chooses to immerse his camera in the

---

[18] Baudouin Dupret, *Practices of Truth*, p. 141.

newsroom of *El Watan*. Created in 1990 by journalists who left the official state newspaper *El Moudjahid*, *El Watan* was, at the time of filming, regarded as an independent newspaper working to promote democracy and prepared to cover the Algerian political opposition. The paper had a circulation of 140,000, according to its director Omar Belhouchet.[19] The title of the film, *Contre-pouvoirs*, refers to the press as one of the pillars of democracy, its mission to counterbalance state power by providing independent and reliable news.

The newsroom Bensmaïl films is at once a site of freedom and one where the country's *lack* of liberty is clearly visible. Since 1989, Algerian print media have benefited from new legislation that allowed multipartyism and legalized media outlets related to the new political parties. The Algerian press survived during the Civil War, despite numerous attacks that targeted journalists and censorship imposed by the ministry of information during the conflict. *El Moudjahid* remains the organ of the FLN, *El Djeich* speaks for the Army. The daily *El Watan* and *El Khabar* are considered liberal newspapers, practicing independent journalism vis-à-vis the state and Algeria's political parties. Bensmaïl's first intention was to film both newsrooms, but after a few days filming at *El Khabar,* he concluded that the journalists were not acting as freely and naturally in front of the camera as he had hoped. He thus decided to focus his film on the *El Watan's* newsroom. He had begun with these two papers, in part, in the awareness that despite nominal freedom of the press, the state might still exercise censorship indirectly through its control of the printing houses. It was for that reason that *El Khabar* and *El Watan* had decided to co-own their printing house as early as August 2003. Bensmaïl therefore inserts scenes of the newspaper being printed throughout the documentary: these transition shots refer to the daily operation of printing but—much as the bus is always also November 1 in *La Chine*—here the presses of the transition shots also remind viewers of the freedom reclaimed by *El Watan*.

The relative freedom of the journalist is the subject of many scenes in the film. As a diminished and invisible Bouteflika campaigns for a fourth term, two journalists endlessly debate their views on the country and their political convictions. The spectator witnesses the editor working with a cartoonist to find the right way of representing the surreal situation

[19] Belhouchet mentioned the circulation figure during the International Film Festival Amsterdam in November 2018. https://soundcloud.com/idfapodcast. Accessed June 14, 2022.

Algerian voters now face, as they are asked to vote for an invisible candidate. In several scenes, Bensmaïl follows the experienced journalist and writer Moustapha Benfodil, who is covering the presidential election; Benfodil is also an active member of the movement Barakat, which gathers activists who oppose Bouteflika's candidacy. Thus, Benfodil both covers the elections and attends protests organized by the movement; he coordinates a press conference where he and other Barakat members express their disappointment with the election results but promise to keep fighting. The camera captures protesters being arrested, even as others continue to shout pro-democracy slogans. Each of these scenes shows that opposition politics, freedom of expression, and freedom of the press are in some degree tolerated—and they are tolerated precisely because the actual political situation has changed little since Bensmaïl filmed *Le Grand jeu in 2004*. Bouteflika's clan is still in power.

Although Algeria still plays the "grand jeu" of electoral politics, the de facto paralysis of the political system has consequences for the press. Any freedom that the spectator witnesses is nuanced by other scenes, elements of contextualization and by transitional shots throughout the film. If we see multiple shots of newspapers moving rapidly off *El Watan*'s independently owned presses, these are, in turn, counterbalanced by repeated images of stasis. Bensmaïl repeatedly films the daily's director Omar Belhouchet running on a treadmill, and the shots work as a metaphor for the impasse that Belhouchet and his newspaper are trying to escape in a country where Bouteflika's power has increased and freedom of speech is increasingly at risk. During one transitional sequence, the sounds of the treadmill and the printing press are indistinguishably overlaid, suggesting that both are literally and figuratively running to nowhere.

An important storyline in the film is *El Watan*'s effort to acquire its own building. At the beginning of the documentary, the filmmaker reminds the audience that since the *décennie noire*, or "black decade"—the Civil War of the 1990s—*El Watan* has been located in *La Maison de la presse*, a public institution that welcomes different news outlets. The anticipated move to a new building symbolizes a further step toward independence for *El Watan*. But construction started in 2001, and there is little indication it will be finished soon. Faithful to his immersive approach, Bensmaïl gives the audience no information that would explain why construction is taking so long; the transitional shots imply, however, a never-ending, Sisyphean endeavor, mirroring the shots of Belhouchet running and running on his treadmill and yet always finding himself in the same place.

But not all the obstacles Belhouchet must face are metaphorical. In the only scene where the viewer actually sees him move, we follow him on the subway to a meeting with the newspaper's lawyer, Khaled Bourayou. Bensmaïl uses their conversation to show the ongoing risks incurred by the newspaper and its journalists. One of the paper's leading columnists, Chawki Amari, and Omar Belhouchet as his director have been charged with defaming the *Wali* (Governor) of Jijel; the lawyer explains that both have been sentenced to two months in prison and a 100,000 DA fine. Belhouchet regrets that the Algerian authorities cannot tell the difference between news and opinion and thus reminds the audience that freedom of speech cannot be achieved completely as long as government authorities continue to threaten and intimidate journalists.

The apparent freedom that reigns in the *El Watan* newsroom is thus ultimately revealed as an illusion, as the degree of journalistic freedom that exists in Algeria has little impact on what happens in the political arena. Like the other Bensmaïl documentaries discussed in this chapter, *Contrepouvoirs* tells the story of an Algerian society trying to free itself from paralyzing obstacles imposed by the political system. Together these films offer a valuable understanding of the conditions that would lead many Algerians to take to the streets a few years later, on the announcement that Bouteflika intended to run for a fifth term. As Bensmaïl summed up during our interview, "It's not enough to show the violence, nor just to cover the news. There is a duty to record the changes, the ideas, the battles—to record a democracy that is fighting to emerge but that is nevertheless still being built day by day."

References

Brahimi, Denise. *Regards sur les cinémas du Maghreb*. Paris: Éditions Petra, 2016.
Ciment, James. *Algeria: The Fundamentalist Challenge*. New York: Facts on File, 1997.
Dupret, Baudouin. *Practices of Truth: An Ethnomethodological Inquiry into Arab Contexts*. Philadelphia: John Benjamins Publishing Company, 2011.
Harbi, Mohammed. *1954. La guerre commence en Algérie*. Bruxelles: Éditions Complexe, 1984.
Harbi, Mohammed and Gilles Meynier. *Le FLN : Documents et histoire (1954–1962)*. Paris: Fayard, 2004.

Remaoun, Hassen. « L'enseignement de l'Histoire de la Guerre de libération nationale à travers une lecture des manuels scolaires algériens », *Internationale Schulbuchforschung, Algerien, Frankreich und der Algerienkrieg, France and the Algerian War*, vol.26 No. 1, 2004: 59-74.

Wallenbrock, Nicole Beth. *The Franco-Algerian War Through a Twenty-First Century Lens. Film and History.* London: Bloomsbury Academic, 2020.

CHAPTER 4

Hassen Ferhani: Margins, Beauty, and Truth

Mentir-vrai—Louis Aragon

"We don't lie, but neither do we come upon the truth." This line is repeated several times in Hassen Ferhani's first feature documentary, *Dans ma tête un rond-point* (2015), spoken by 'Ammou (little uncle), one of the film's main characters. As mentioned in our interview, Ferhani considered using this sentiment as the documentary's title but eventually settled on a shorter phrase from another character who expresses how lost he feels in terms of a "roundabout in his head." 'Ammou's comment on truth and lies nevertheless captures the heart of Ferhani's cinematographic project, a project that seeks to get as close as possible to reality while always recognizing that truth in its entirety is unattainable. A documentary or any film, says Ferhani, can reveal a truth but not all the truth(s).

Like Malek Bensmaïl (Chap. 3) with whom he worked as first assistant for the documentary *Contre-pouvoirs* (2015), Ferhani privileges an immersive approach to filmmaking with a deep attention to sound and to the utterances of his subjects. His documentaries have a sequential organization and tend to tell an overarching story about either a single place or one specific character. The documentary's narrative is comprised of non-mediated, real-time scenes in which the characters are filmed in what appear to be natural situations. The characters' voices thus give the impression of transparency. Upon further inspection, however, we see that there is in fact significant mediation through scripted scenes. Ferhani's conviction, from the earliest stages of his career, is that in every film—whether fiction or documentary—each character plays a role. And yet he also

© The Author(s), under exclusive license to Springer Nature Switzerland AG 2023
M. Belkaïd, *From Outlaw to Rebel*, Palgrave Studies in Arab Cinema, https://doi.org/10.1007/978-3-031-19157-2_4

believes that filmmaking allows for some truth to be revealed. As Stella Bruzzi describes in what she calls "performative documentaries," performance is seen not as a means of invalidating the documentary pursuit, but of getting more efficaciously to the truth the filmmaker is seeking.[1] He is close to what Aline Caillet and Fréderic Pouillaude call a "poetics of factuality and singular existence."[2] There is in Ferhani's style both playfulness and fidelity to reality, an attention to marginal destinies and spaces and to beauty and aesthetic achievement.

Immersing himself in the spaces and people he films, Ferhani chooses to be playful with reality, exhibiting an exceptional delicacy and gentleness through his compositions. He will often use a quiet exchange of glances or words to elicit a sense of intimacy between viewer and viewed, reminding us that the films are the product of his own mind and gaze. Ferhani develops and affirms this aesthetic approach—static camera long takes and direct-to-camera interviews—in one film after another. The short film *Le Vol du 104* (2008) that he presented at the end of his summer training at La Fémis (*École Nationale Supérieure des Métiers de l'Image et du Son*) in Paris, embodies all these commitments in his filmmaking. The film is a series of improvised and scripted situations in which Ferhani and his crew ask his building's inhabitants if they know the whereabouts of a plant which belonged to Esmelinda, the building's custodian, and has been stolen. It is clear to the viewer that some situations are scripted even if the theft actually did occur.

As Ferhani explains in our interview, the documentary form allows him also to have more financial independence vis-à-vis the Algerian state and public funds.[3] Narimane Mari (Chap. 1), his producer since 2013, is committed to helping young Algerian filmmakers craft their cinematographic universe without worrying about state expectations. Mari created her own

[1] Stella Bruzzi, *New Documentary*. Routledge, 2006, p.153–154.

[2] Aline Caillet and Fréderic Pouillaude (dir.), *Un Art documentaire. Enjeux esthétiques, politiques et éthiques*, Presses Universitaires de Rennes, 2017, p. 13.

[3] Interview conducted in February 2019. All subsequent quotes from Ferhani will be from this interview.

production company *Aller-Retour* with this purpose in mind.[4] After years of producing films in France, she sought to help Algerian filmmakers. She met Hassen Ferhani at a festival in Spain where he was presenting his film *Tarzan, Don Quichotte et nous* (2013). Ferhani recalls Mari asking him what he needed to make his next film, and he gave an answer she loved: "I just need a camera and a sound engineer!" Their collaboration was born at the moment.

Ferhani's modest financial requirements and his access to private production support combine to enable his control over his films and make the filmmaking process more manageable. Fittingly, his embrace of modest means of production consciously flies in the face of everything the Algerian state and the Algerian state-funded cinema have perennially stood for. Under President Bouteflika's reign, the national cinema, guided by a new neoliberal logic, favored big productions about the colonial past. Though *Dans ma tête un rond-point* (2015) received 40,000 euros toward post-production costs from the Algerian Ministry of Culture, the film received more money from Qatar (Doha Institute) and Lebanon (Arab Funds for Art and Culture, or AFAC), and had an entire budget of only 90,000 euros.

And yet this financial restraint does not keep Ferhani from producing images that are aesthetically and cinematographically compelling. His attention to color, framing, light, and the exploration of spaces as true characters in his documentaries, places his filmmaking somewhere between *films d'auteur* and the Algerian tradition of popular cinema—inherited from Merzak Allouache and others. To depict Algerian society, he chooses reality and allows himself to play with it and even transfigure it aesthetically, affirming his subjectivity while trying to get as close as possible to his characters' truth through performance.

---

[4] Narimane Mari began her film career in 2001 by producing films. Since 2006 she has produced within the company *Centrale Électrique* and then *Aller-retour* of which she is the founding member. Her company has produced both Ferhani's feature films and Djamel Kerkar's *Atllal* (2017). She has also directed *Loubia Hamra* (2013) and *Le Fort des fous* (2017). She is currently producing the works of two Algerian women documentary makers: Amira Louadah and Bahia Benchikh El Fegoune.

Disrupting Official Discourse: *Afric Hotel* (2010)[5]

In his documentary, *Afric Hotel* (2010), Ferhani questions Algeria's official discourse, explicitly and in great depth. *Afric Hotel* is indeed a much more immersive work than *Tarzan, Don Quichotte et nous* (2013) that explored the Cervantès neighborhood of Algiers where two characters in a car interacted with inhabitants in a playful yet fleeting manner. In *Afric Hotel*, he focuses on the trajectory of three main characters living in the same locale. Ibrahim, Adam, and Ismael are immigrants from sub-Saharan Africa living and working illegally in Algeria. In our conversations, Ferhani offered that this film was conceived as an explicit rebuttal to Algerian state messaging surrounding the 2009 Pan-African Festival. In 2009 the Algerian authorities organized a second Pan-African Festival, 50 years after the famous festival of 1969. Ferhani had seen William Klein's documentary *Festival Panafricain d'Alger 1969* (1969) and wanted to gather a team of filmmakers to cover the event just as Klein had done for his film. But this time Ferhani didn't want to document the festival itself.[6] Instead, he wanted to film the harsh reality of the lives of sub-Saharan African migrants in Algeria. His friend Nabil Djedouani enthusiastically answered the call, and they worked together on the film.

While the state was officially celebrating Africa with this second edition of the Pan-African Festival, the two filmmakers sought to show how migrants from sub-Saharan Africa were marginalized in Algeria and impacted by racism. During my conversations with Ferhani, he recalls that he learned a lot about documentary-making during the shooting. He came to understand the importance of taking the time to get to know the characters, and he and Djedouani quickly developed the idea that they needed to make those characters the active subjects of the film, rather than objects of the camera's gaze. The two filmmakers were not allowed to enter the hotel as the rules forbade guests, but they wanted the audience to see how the migrants lived. Therefore, the documentary starts with footage of the migrant's hotel room, filmed by Ibrahim who forgot to turn on the sound button while filming, and the scene is thus silent. While the filming might seem technically and cinematically ragged with jumpy images imperfectly framed, the silence intensifies the viewer's sense of

---

[5] *Afric Hotel* is available on YouTube: https://www.youtube.com/watch?v=dE6_FPcbd7c. Accessed June 16, 2022.

[6] Algerian Filmmaker Salem Brahimi directed *Africa is back* (2010), a state funded documentary about the festival of 2009.

being totally immersed in the migrant's life and reality. The two directors, Ferhani and Djedouani, decided to insert this scene to show a hidden place and the conditions of scarcity in migrant life at the hotel that gives the documentary its name. The contrast between the noise and excess of the festival and the silence in the hotel is arresting; it is then further underscored as we hear, in a subsequent scene, music and fireworks from the festival in the background, signaling a celebration of Africa that is taking place nearby.

The documentary's subtext addresses the imagined community with which Algerians are supposed to identify. This is, officially, a community built not only on principles of solidarity and equality between its Algerian members[7] but also on the extension of that solidarity and egalitarianism to all people belonging to the so-called Third World. The official nationalist discourse has thus worked on two levels, imagining a united Algerian community and an equally united Third World community: this is the vision celebrated in the Pan-African Festival. And if parts of this discourse are internalized by Algerians—who especially in the 1970s considered their country as the "Mecca for revolutionaries[8]" and leaders of the Non-Aligned movement—this discourse is at odds with the actual inequalities existing between Algerians and migrants from sub-Saharan Africa. The official version of harmony runs counter to the long-standing practices of exploitation and feelings of superiority toward sub-Saharan Africans that are firmly part of Algerian history and culture. During our interview, Ferhani recalled that when the film was first released in Algeria, some spectators were displeased by the inference of this racism towards migrants and its ability to reveal the paradoxes of maintaining an official discourse that contradicts social realities.

Against the backdrop of national exhibits at the festival—Ferhani and Djedouani's film offers its own "exhibits" of migrant living spaces, migrant workplaces, and smaller spaces (such as elevators) where migrants find themselves in close proximity to coworkers and neighbors. Ultimately, the film questions the façade of a joyful festival that celebrates a unified Africa while migrants from the rest of the continent live in such difficult

---

[7] "Finally, it is imagined as a community, because regardless of the actual inequality and exploitation that may prevail in each, the nation is always conceived as a deep horizontal comradeship," in Benedict Anderson, *Imagined Communities. Reflections on the Origin and Spread of Nationalism.* Verso, 2002, p. 7.

[8] See Jeffrey James, Byrne, *Mecca of Revolution: Algeria, Decolonization, and the Third World Order*, Oxford University Press, 2016.

conditions in today's Algeria. It allows the audience to gain a deeper knowledge of the daily life of men they rarely see on screen, and conveys feelings of empathy, making it perhaps easier for viewers to understand and feel the daily racism that Ibrahim, Ismael, and Adam must face.

Some of the Algerian characters appearing in *Afric Hotel* expressed a desire that the documentary portray a positive image of the country. In the elevator, Ismael's workplace, one interlocutor offers that the documentary is a nice idea—so that spectators can see how well Ismael and his friends are treated. The film's Algerian characters state over and over that Algeria is a welcoming country; they also insist on the superiority of their country over other African countries. This dismissive attitude turns to outright racism when Ismael explains to a neighbor that the camera in the elevator is filming them as part of a documentary project: the neighbor asks if the documentary is about animals.

Racism toward sub-Saharans—and racism in general—goes against a glorified vision of the country instilled by the Algerian state and interiorized by the citizens. Racism may be evident and widespread, but officially it does not, or should not, exist. It is difficult, both nationally and personally, to face such a crucial failure of the narrative of a united and heroic nation that overcame colonial racism and thus epidemic racism is denied. In *Afric Hotel*, Ferhani and Djedouani document the impact of a constructed official discourse on individual identity. For both filmmakers, what matters most is not the narrative promulgated by the authorities and official media, but the harsh reality lived by the migrants; it is not surprising that Ibrahim compares the conditions in which he works to slavery. The official nationalist discourse that presents Algeria as a uniquely welcoming African country has shaped the minds of Algerians who now find themselves trapped between the irreconcilable positions of solidarity and superiority.

Exploring the Margins

After *Afric Hotel*, Ferhani brought his immersive approach from the world of migrants to the city's working class. He was convinced that he needed to explore further the paradoxes of Algerian society by documenting marginal spaces as an implicit challenge to heroic narratives of national unity. In *Dans ma tête un rond-point* (2015), Ferhani follows a group of men working in a slaughterhouse in the city of Algiers. Ferhani recalls that during a stay in Algeria, he entered the slaughterhouse on a whim after a meal in a restaurant nearby. He understood instantly that he needed to film this place and felt so even more strongly when he learned that the building would soon be demolished and forgotten. Ferhani edited the final film from a total of 60 hours of footage. In describing the initial inspiration for the film, Ferhani explains in our conversations that he had been thinking about filming the Algerian working class—who, like the sub-Saharan migrants of *Hotel Afric* (2010), are in his opinion underrepresented in Algerian media and cinema. Film critic Mouny Berrah confirms this, writing that the working class is the group that is most noticeably absent from Algerian cinema in which the image of national identity is conveyed through characters and individuals rather than through social classes.[9]

In a country still recovering from the 1990s Civil War, the slaughterhouse's environment—with slaughtered animals and blood everywhere—was for many Algerians highly evocative of recent traumas of the Civil War. Ferhani works to get his audience to identify as fully as possible with the subjects that he films and to look at those subjects' lived experience closely without indulging in voyeurism or intruding on subjects' privacy. An earlier example of lived experience through multiple stories is his short film, *Les Baies d'Alger* (2006), which he presents as an *audio-scopie* of the city where he was born. The film is composed of 15 sketches in which we hear characters without seeing them, as they talk about their daily lives and mundane topics such as their bills, the best hairdresser in town, a shaky business, or a love story. The themes tackled by *Les Baies d'Alger* (2006) are those that Ferhani's characters will explore more deeply in his subsequent documentaries. As Marie-Pierre Ullola writes, Ferhani is "forever filming *his* Algiers."[10] The movie wants to convey the feel of a documentary, with camera movements and zooms signaling the transitions where we as viewers are transported from one place to another and to what is going on in different parts of the city.

In *Dans ma tête un rond-point*, certain characters can be considered the protagonists of the documentary. There is the inseparable duo Youcef and his sidekick *El qbayli*, a nickname that connects him to the region of Kabylia. There is the old man, Uncle Ali, who has been working in the slaughterhouse since 1945, who recites poems from memory, and who

[9] Mouny Berrah, Victor Bachy, Mohand Ben Salma et Férid Boughedir (dir.), *CinémAction Cinémas du Maghreb*. Revue trimestrielle, No. 14, Spring 1981, p.46.

[10] Marie-Pierre Ulloa, « Fi Rassi/ Dans ma tête un Rond-point », *Journal of Islamic and Muslim Studies*, Vol.1, No.2 (November 2016), p. 91.

lives in a small room with a mattress on the floor. There is also 'Ammou (an affectionate form of the Arabic word which means uncle), the middle-aged man who speaks in riddles and infuses the documentary with a sense of mystery; and finally the old man who haunts the slaughterhouse surroundings with his cryptic utterances. Ferhani also interacts with a gamut of other workers who talk about their lives and express their dreams and their fears.

143 rue du desert (2019), Ferhani's second full-length documentary, focuses again on a single interior space, a rest stop on the Pan-African Highway, which connects Algiers to the Sahara and the city of Tamanrasset, farther to the south.[11] In this film the primary subject is Malika, a 60-year-old woman who owns the coffee shop. Once again, Ferhani spent two months filming Malika's daily life and her interactions with passing customers, primarily male drivers who stop in for drinks and food. Malika lives and works by herself in what might optimistically be called a "café": a one-room shack with two tables. The walls are white, with no decorations, no signs of comfort, emphasizing that the place is much more a *lieu de passage* than a place to stay and enjoy a good meal or drink. Unlike the chorus of characters making up *Dans ma tête un rond-point*, Malika can be considered the main character. She "reigns over her kingdom," as a tourist from Poland puts it, smiling into Ferhani's camera, when she learns that Malika means "queen" in Arabic. But Malika's interactions with the clients who stop in and talk with her are an important part of the film. Some of them know Malika and care about her. Others are curious, and sometimes even nosy, about her surprising lifestyle.

In both films, Ferhani uses neither a voiceover nor elements of contextualization to explain the circumstances in which he starts filming. That decision, of course, is a way of giving priority to images but also to the characters' stories. Ferhani offers the audience a narrative that emerges through editorial and aesthetic choices, the stories of marginalized people who become the film's protagonists. The documentaries have a sequential organization. In each scene a character or a group of characters speak about various topics, and some are filmed in what seem to be natural situations while others are filmed as direct-to-camera interviews. The film portrays characters who are facing many obstacles and even an external threat that is emphasized mainly in the transitional scenes.

---

[11] *143, rue du désert* is available on DVD.

In *Dans ma tête un rond-point* (2015), the transitional scenes realistically portray the physical conditions in which the slaughterhouse workers do their jobs. Ferhani takes a decidedly neutral stance vis-à-vis the animals' treatment and the violence they endure, suggesting their inevitable fate pre and post-mortem. The audience can see cows or sheep entering at one end, and cuts of meat and hides leaving at the other end. In between, workers hang up the animals on hooks, disassemble them, process the meat, and stuff it into trucks or barrels.

The slaughterhouse was built in 1929, during the French colonization and spreads out over 24,000 square meters with various buildings—sheds, rooms, and workshops—which could "process" up to 500 cattle and 5000 sheep per day. It employed about a hundred people along with numerous transporters, breeders, horse dealers, and butchers who come to deliver, sell, or buy. In 2011, the government decided to demolish it and to make way for a parliamentary complex that would include new buildings for the Senate and the National Assembly. Modern slaughterhouses were to be built on the capital's outskirts to meet the needs of the city and adapt to new production and health standards. In March 2014, Khalida Toumi, then Minister of Culture, issued a decree, published in the Official Journal of March 23, 2014, stating that the Algiers slaughterhouses were pending classification as national cultural heritage and not to be demolished; this decree was canceled, and the demolition eventually happened in February 2019, four years after Ferhani's film was released and a few days before the beginning of the *Hirak* movement. Ferhani never explicitly mentions the planned demolition, but many transitional scenes in the documentary insist on the neglected aspect of the place and the outdated nature of the equipment, conveying the idea of a place about to disappear. Many shots show the location as clearly crumbling and in very poor condition, with plaster and painting falling away, details that express aesthetically the workers' own palpable feelings of exhaustion and the demolition to come.

Malika's rest stop is also threatened, but this time Ferhani renders this threat more explicit to the audience. Malika and her guests mention several times that a man is about to open a new gas station next door that will also be a restaurant. Malika seems worried with this new competition while her costumers reassure her. One man reminds Malika that only God can take away what he gave when she expresses her fear of losing her livelihood:

– *They are taking my bread and butter*

> – *They can't do that. Only He (his index points to the sky) can do that. He gives and takes.*

Despite her clients' encouragement, Malika expresses several times her willingness to leave the place, but on her terms, and without her family. Ferhani amplifies the suspense of Malika's (ultimately unresolved) decision, with a series of transitional scenes, showing the evolution of the construction next door, with shots of the building from beginning to end, and a final scene in which the station is connected to electricity and all the lights turned on.

Malika must adapt to this new competition in much the way that the workers of the slaughterhouse must face the destruction of their workplace. Ferhani chooses in both films to tell the stories with characters as heroes facing obstacles and challenges. Toward the end of *Dans ma tête un rond-point*, the national media come to the slaughterhouse to film the busy run-up to the celebration of Eid. 'Ammou comments ironically about the national media: "They only come here during Eid," letting the audience know that the workplace and its hundred workers are forgotten the rest of the year. 'Ammou then adds the cryptic sentence he repeats throughout the film: "We don't lie, but neither do we come upon the truth." This time, he applies it specifically to the national media, giving us perhaps the key to what he meant all along: the lies are the official ones Algerians have been told for years, and these are primarily lies of omission that render 'Ammou and all his colleagues invisible.

Ferhani's documentaries point out that the subjects he is filming are the true heroes by implicitly comparing them to other leading figures who are portrayed in his films as shadowy or fading figures. His camera, in *Dans ma tête un rond-point*, lingers on a drawing of President Liamine Zeroual on one interior wall of the slaughterhouse, and then on a ripped poster of President Abdelaziz Bouteflika. In *143 rue du désert*, the national leader is even more literally a ghost, since the only political figure mentioned is former President Houari Boumediene, who died in 1978. Malika and one of her customers recall President Boumediene nostalgically for all that he has achieved for the country. We even hear a portion of a speech given by the former president, after a scene in which the customer had proudly shown off his picture, which he uses as the wallpaper on his mobile device (Fig. 4.1).

Malika's nostalgia and the shadowy figures pasted on the walls of the slaughterhouse signal one of contemporary's Algeria greatest challenges

Fig. 4.1 Malika and a costumer listening to Houari Boumediene's speech on a mobile device

after the end of the Civil War. The disenchantment is palpable, and the wounds are still open. The characters of Ferhani's films feel abandoned, as if they don't belong to the Algerian community. Salah, one of the workers in the slaughterhouse, gets drunk one night and summarizes the desire to grab back control of his destiny, saying: "I am in my country, I am not colonized. I don't fear the state." He knows very well that he is not completely free: he is in his country, but in a country that President Bouteflika has ruled for a fourth term despite the two-term limit in the original constitution. Ferhani's filmmaking denounces this central crisis by juxtaposing the harsh conditions in which his characters live, and the omnipresent iron bars that constrain their lives and depict the characters as imprisoned.

Youcef says it best with the sentence that will give the film its title. Having a roundabout in his head is a way for him to convey the idea that he feels stuck in his life and doesn't know which way to choose among the 99 paths that he struggles with in his mind. In a later scene he narrows the possibilities he has to only two: either suicide or illegal immigration. Youssef and the slaughterhouse workers are like the caged birds that Ferhani uses as a metaphor throughout the film in several transitional scenes. All his characters are misfits, abandoned to their fates in remote places and marginalized spaces. They experience what Peter Limbrick calls a feeling of dispossession, a sense of impossibility that the film connects to the political space that the men inhabit.[12]

But they also show resilience through their love for poetry and beauty and their praise for a simple life in contrast with the neoliberal policy put in place during the Bouteflika years. Each is searching for a truth, be it historical or spiritual, and Ferhani consciously avoids wretchedness in the way he depicts their lives and tells their stories. The filmmaker wants his audience to enter the places he is filming with curiosity and respect. In the two documentary features, Ferhani has reached a level of maturity in his filmmaking, building his unique aesthetic through immersion. The films ensure for the viewer a sense of closeness and even intimacy with the characters. The daily life of the character matters much more than any preconceived narrative of the filmmaker or the viewer.

Ferhani constructs an experience that is fully and foremost sensorial. The immersion in Ferhani's cinema induces a synesthesia: from sight, to sound, to a third sensory or cognitive pathway. The angst conveyed by the colors and the sounds Ferhani captures, the melancholy evoked by the songs, help the spectators to realize that each place Ferhani films is a metonym of Algeria, expressive of the country's recent past, making plainly visible truths the state had left invisible. In these two later movies, there is a near obsessive attention to color. Red is a dominant color in *Dans ma tête un rond-point*, and Ferhani manages to show its importance not only by filming the blood of the slaughterhouse but also by juxtaposing that blood-red with other reds. In the film's opening scene, we see a long shot of the slaughterhouse's exterior, and then the title appears printed over the image in bold, red capital letters. Since the film is punctuated by static shots that frame different objects—chairs, tables, or a ladder leaning up against a wall—the color reappears throughout the movie on red-painted walls, coat hangers, on brick roofs, on characters' clothes or bags (Fig. 4.2). He also contrasts those reds against blue. Blue is indeed another dominant color throughout the film, as Ferhani shot mainly at night. This second color emphasizes the nocturnal atmosphere and contributes to the spectator's sense that this exploration of the slaughterhouse is unauthorized.

Set in the Sahara, *143 rue du désert* is more a daytime film. It is then no surprise that the color of sand is dominant in this documentary. Many

---

[12] Peter Limbrick, "Spaces of Dispossession: Experiments with the Real in Contemporary Algerian Cinema", in Viola Shafik (dir.), *Documentary Filmmaking in the Middle East and North Africa*. The American University in Cairo Press, p. (to be published in August 23).

Fig. 4.2 Youcef leaning toward a TV screen in front of red-painted walls in *Dans ma tête un rond-point*

shots are an explicit homage to John Ford's Westerns with frames and scenes that show Malika caught in a metaphysical situation. Ferhani's *143 rue du désert* shares with John Ford's western films aesthetic features but also some of their recurrent themes like memory and loss, the plight of outsiders and the tragedy of a family break-up.[13] In one arresting scene, the camera catches Malika's dog running along the road. The dog's color is very close to the sand's color beneath her as she runs, and Malika tries in vain to call her back. This moment of cinematic bliss when light, natural elements, characters, and animals converge in creating a beautiful palette of colors is one of Ferhani's signatures. It echoes the opening scene of *Dans ma tête un rond-point*, in which Uncle Ali appears for the first time and recites a rhymed epic poem. In that scene he is dressed in blue, and behind him the sunset sky offers an astonishing palette of colors from blue to pink; the framing makes the scene appear painterly. Uncle Ali also closes the movie, walking toward his apartment, gently saluting the film crew, in a dark blue light.

The filmmaker also pays particular attention to sounds. *Fi Rassi*'s opening scene shows a young worker turning the handle of a winch, with an

[13] Jeffrey Richards, *The Lost Worlds of John Ford*. Bloomsbury Academic, 2020.

intensely unpleasant metallic sound that will haunt the whole documentary. As Peter Limbrick writes: "The soundtrack captures the squeak of the winch as it turns the cable, hoisting something that is still held offscreen, beyond our vision. We see cause, but not effect (…)."[14] This sound alludes to the machinery of torture and, by extension, to the sounds of torment and death. It portends all the sounds we will hear during the documentary of animals in agony, or animals refusing instinctively and stubbornly to move toward their executioners.

Death is present everywhere in the slaughterhouse and the soundtrack conveys an atmosphere of angst—angst as felt by the animals being led to slaughter, as carried in turn by the workers, and by extension as experienced by the audience. As Peter Limbrick shows, this makes the film "expressionistic to the extent that the external qualities of its *mise-en-scène* are indicative of the state of mind of its characters".[15] This heavy atmosphere is palpable from the movie's opening, in a workplace that is scheduled to be demolished, leaving hundreds of people unemployed; the weight intensifies as we realize that the slaughterhouse is in some sense a metonym of post–Civil War Algeria.

The viewer is so immersed in the setting of Ferhani's film that they can hear even sounds that are actually inaudible in the soundtrack. In one nighttime scene, custodians are distracted by a frightening sound. The viewer can't hear the sound itself—the custodians have been watching television with the volume turned up high. But the fear is so palpable, and the focus is so tightly on the characters' experience that the audience can readily imagine the frightening sounds that might be heard in a slaughterhouse at night. We "hear" the sound as we see the characters respond to it.

The aesthetic choice to use only diegetic music in both documentaries reinforces the immersive experience. In *Dans ma tête un rond-point*, the spectator hears only the music that characters listen to on the radio or their mobile phones—or even that they sing themselves, as when Youcef hums while working. Most of the songs are standards of raï (Cheb Azzedine, Cheb Hasni, Cheikh El Hamel) and chaabi (Amar Ezahi) two popular genres in Algeria. Youcef's friend, in the middle of a heated conversation, starts singing to express one of his ideas, and in a very touching scene,

---

[14] Peter Limbrick, "Spaces of Dispossession: Experiments with the Real in Contemporary Algerian Cinema", in Viola Shafik (dir.), *Documentary Filmmaking*. p. 314.

[15] Peter Limbrick, "Spaces of Dispossession: Experiments with the Real in Contemporary Algerian Cinema", in Viola Shafik (dir.), *Documentary Filmmaking*, p. 314.

Youcef who also knows the lyrics, joins in. In both documentaries, the score for the final credits is sung by one of the characters: Youcef sings a song of Cheb Hasni *Ana jamais nensa l'passé* (I will never forget the past) about an impossible love, while Malika is filmed singing *El Menfi*, an ancient song about exile and pain, themes that are clearly specific to the characters' stories. Ferhani invites characters to sing their own songs, much as they tell their stories in their own words.

In *143 rue du désert*, for the first time, Ferhani uses extradiegetic sound. In the opening scene the audience can hear a traditional song from the region of Kabylia, performed by singer Taos Amrouche. The song immediately conveys a sense of meditative contemplation, because it is an incantation in honor of a dead man. It also deeply roots the film in Algeria, with a reference to a heritage that is not always valued by the state, because the singer's family in Kabylia was converted to Christianity during the colonial period and because, as an activist for the Amazigh cause, she does not match nationalist criteria for artistic recognition. There is a parallel to be drawn between Taos Amrouche and Malika. Amrouche is artistically marginalized as is Malika geographically and socially. But Ferhani doesn't want his movies to be restricted to the Algerian context, and he uses a piece from Brian Eno's album *My Life in the Bush of Ghosts* (1981). The song, called *Quran*, features Algerian men chanting the Qur'an over an electronic sound backing track. Ferhani uses the piece to stress the contemplative and spiritual atmosphere of Malika's desert road stop and how that place belongs to a global cultural context. Very precise work on sound makes the song appear as if it's part of the surroundings and the shop's sound environment. Ferhani asked his sound engineer to introduce the song immediately after a scene where Malika is trying to listen to the radio: the transition is so smooth that the ear can't immediately discern the difference between the radio's metallic sound and the instruments being played in Eno's song. Close to Malika's shop there is a Zaouia, a place of pilgrimage that is mentioned several times either by Malika or by pilgrims heading there. Malika's solitude and her demeanor suggest that, consciously or not, she is acting as a saint and that her shop could be considered as her very own Zaouia.

The immersive aesthetic creates an impression—or perhaps an illusion—of authenticity and editing choices are in sync with cinematic choices. The slaughterhouse workers' nights and Malika's days are full of downtime where nothing happens. Long still shots expand time and put the spectator in the characters' shoes. But Ferhani in his quest for truth allows a certain playfulness with reality. He often mentions Louis Aragon's expression of *mentir vrai*[16] (to lie truthfully) as the way he conceives filmmaking. He appears occasionally in his films, either as a shadow or even a voice asking questions. In *143 rue du desert* when Malika speaks with the tourist from Poland, he tries to help and translates the words of Malika in English. He makes a mistake by mixing the verbs "buy" and "sell" and when I asked him why he kept the scene despite the error, he said laughing: "I kept the scene because it's how it happened; my English is bad and I didn't want to conceal it and what happened is not lost in translation". His presence, even though discreet, is a way to remind the audience that the films are the product of his own gaze and even if they are close to a certain reality, this reality is filtered through Ferhani's lens.

In *143 rue du desert*, he goes a step further by transforming what he sees into his own narrative. He indeed adds a new component, introducing two actors who interact with Malika in scenes that to a certain extent blur the edges between documentary and fiction. In a first sequence, the author and actor Chawki Ammari (who introduced Malika to Ferhani) is filmed with Malika, with both enacting a scene in which Ammari is supposedly in prison. Ammari stands outside the road stop, behind a window with bars and calls Malika to the parlor; she immediately starts to play along and pretends to be a mother visiting her son in prison. When a costumer enters, Ammari keeps acting as if he were in jail and in need of a lawyer, but Malika ends up laughing, trying to stop Ammari and reassuring the costumer by explaining that the crew is here to film her.

Ferhani also asked actor Samir El Hakim who had appeared previously in Ferhani's *Tarzan, Don Quichotte et nous* (2013) to come and stop at the road stop. Malika, according to Ferhani, is not aware that he is an actor. Ferhani and El Hakim agreed to act as if they didn't know each other and while he is at Malika's shop, he explains that he is looking for his brother who has been missing for years. Malika then tells him that she also lost her daughter who was taken from her years ago. When El Hakim leaves, Malika looks at Ferhani's camera and says that she is sure that the man is a liar and that's why she also lied to him with the story of a daughter that she never had. While El Hakim might be a recognizable public figure for a portion of the Algerian audience, he is likely unknown to most viewers and Ferhani never reveals in the film that the scene was staged without

---

[16] *Le Mentir vrai* is the title of a collection of short stories by French writer Louis Aragon. See Louis Aragon, *Le Mentir-Vrai*. nrf, Gallimard, 1980.

Malika's knowledge; he includes it like the other scenes as a natural situation. It was a way for Ferhani to address in his film the sensitive topic of missing persons in contemporary Algeria. To this day, the cases of thousands missing persons who disappeared mainly during the Civil War, are estimated at between 8000 and 10,000 and remain unsolved.[17] By asking Samir El Hakim to improvise a story about a lost brother, Ferhani injected fiction, soon joined by Malika who intuitively and uncannily decided to lie and create a story in response to El Hakim's.

Ammari's and El Hakim's scenes are a way for Ferhani to signal that even if the material of his documentary is "reality," it is put together by his particular mind and sensitivity and shaped by his own interests, memories and values. Whence his discomfort with the distinction between documentary and fiction as clear-cut opposites. He considers himself first and foremost a cinematographer and a storyteller that might be lucky enough to sometimes stumble on the truth. It's not surprising that Hassen Ferhani says that he is now ready to direct a fictional work, most likely seeking a different notion of "truth" that acknowledges the construction of his own imagined stories and characters.

References

Anderson, Benedict. *Imagined Communities. Reflections on the Origin and Spread of Nationalism.* London, New York: Verso, 2002.

Berrah, Mouny and Bachy, Victor and Ben Salma, Mohand and Boughedir Férid, CinémAction (dir). *Cinémas du Maghreb.* Revue trimestrielle- N 14, Spring 1981.

Bruzzi, Stella. *New Documentary, Second Ed.* London and New York: Routledge, 2006.

Byrne, Jeffrey James. *Mecca of Revolution: Algeria, Decolonization, and the Third World Order.* New York: Oxford University Press, 2016.

Caillet, Aline and Fréderic Pouillaude (dir.). *Un Art documentaie. Enjeux esthétiques, politiques et éthiques.* Rennes: Presses Universitaires de Rennes, 2017.

Le Sueur, James D. *Between terror and democracy: Algeria since 1989.* London New York: Zed Book, 2010.

Limbrick, Peter. "Spaces of Dispossession: Experiments with the Real in Contemporary Algerian Cinema", in Viola Shafik (dir.), *Documentary Filmmaking in the Middle East and North Africa,* 2022.

---

[17] James D. Le Sueur, *Between terror and democracy: Algeria since 1989.* Zed Book, 2010, p.93.

Richards, Jeffrey. *The Lost Worlds of John Ford,* London: Bloomsbury Academic, 2020.

Ulloa, Marie-Pierre. « Fi Rassi/ Dans ma tête un Rond-point », *Journal of Islamic and Muslim Studies,* Volume 1, Number2, November 2016, 91-98.

CHAPTER 5

Djamel Kerkar. Past, Present, and Poetry

You shall not be built until you are in ruins.—Yunus Emre

One of the few young Algerian filmmakers who was trained in a film school, Kerkar majored in "writing and directing" at *L'Ecole Supérieure des Arts Visuels de Marrakech* (EASAVM) in Morocco and returned to Algeria after graduation. He began working for other filmmakers, mainly as first assistant. As he said during our interview, he was typically involved in the scouting and casting phases but left the crew as shooting began, because he claimed not to enjoy working on set and felt overwhelmed by the big machinery and crowded film sets.[1] It was during his work on *Et Maintenant ils peuvent venir* (2015), directed by Salem Brahimi, that he met with Hassen Ferhani, who was about to start shooting his documentary *Dans ma tête un rond-point* (2015), set in an Algiers slaughterhouse (Chap. 4). Ferhani was looking for a sound recorder and asked Kerkar if he would be interested. The shooting of *Dans ma tête* confirmed for Kerkar that documentary was his calling, as he had first intuited three years earlier when directing his first short documentary *Archipel* (2012). Kerkar then went on to direct his feature documentary *Atlal* (2017).

In both films, like Malek Bensmaïl (Chap. 3) and Hassen Ferhani (Chap. 4), he uses an immersive approach. He films a single place: a factory in *Archipels* and a village in *Atlal* and the subjects are alternately filmed in non-mediated real-time sequences and in interview-like scenes

---

[1] Interview conducted in May 2019. All subsequent quotes from Kerkar will be from this interview.

© The Author(s), under exclusive license to Springer Nature Switzerland AG 2023
M. Belkaïd, *From Outlaw to Rebel*, Palgrave Studies in Arab Cinema, https://doi.org/10.1007/978-3-031-19157-2_5

with minimal intervention from the filmmaker. Once again, the immersion invokes a keen attention to diegetic sounds and the absence of voiceover and extra-diegetic music. The filmmaker uses a sequential organization in which different characters appear. While Bensmaïl tends to set up a clear context, using inaugural informative texts and sometimes official archival footages, Kerkar dispenses with providing explicit and didactic elements that would help situate the films in a specific political context. This choice is striking for *Atlal*, as the historical background of the Civil War could help the spectator understand why the testimonies gathered in Kerkar's film are so meaningful and important. With no elements of contextualization, the sequencing, the transition shots, and the uses of documents and images belonging to the characters he films allow the audience to stay focused on the personal narratives and the images. The shortcomings of the testimonies, the silences, the sudden revelations, the objects, and the landscapes all convey a fragmented memory that is trying to overcome the trauma of the 1990's conflict.

Women at Work: *Archipel* (2012)

During a workshop at ESAVM, the students had been assigned to work on the theme of "women and femininity." Kerkar recalls that he was at first somewhat annoyed by the topic—North African cinema had addressed this theme so many times, to the point that it seemed hard to avoid repetition and even stereotype. Yet one of the guest speakers, Dalila Ennadre,[2] encouraged the students to search deeply into what the feminine might mean for them personally. Looking through family photos, Kerkar realized that he wanted to talk about labor: he had grown up surrounded by women who worked incessantly, from his grandmother to his mother and his aunts. All these women had worked to the point, it seemed, of sacrificing themselves bodily to their work. Thus, he was determined to make a documentary in which he could film women in their place of work, preferably in a factory.

---

[2] Dalila Ennadre (1968–2020) is a Moroccan documentary maker whose works depict the daily life in Morocco such as *Des murs et des* hommes (2014) on the Casbah of Casablanca. Her last documentary, *Jean Genet, notre père des fleurs* (2020) is an homage to writer and poet Jean Genet who is buried in Morocco and like Ennadre was placed for adoption at a young age.

He eventually decided to document the work of two women in a tannery. The setup is very simple, and Kerkar's choice to film in black and white adds to its sobriety. The actual colors of a tannery workplace can be quite vivid; by choosing black and white, Djamel Kerkar eliminates the colors of the objects the women work on, and thus requires that the spectator focus on the light and the movements of the women themselves. He then explicitly reverses many codes about the male gaze, specifically the conventional codes of the North African context. In her essay "Visual Pleasure and Narrative Cinema," Laura Mulvey has stressed that "as an advanced representation system, the cinema poses questions of the ways the unconscious (formed by the dominant order) structures ways of seeing and pleasure in looking."[3] Among these possible cinematic pleasures is *scopophilia,* the male gaze as enabled by the camera, especially in mainstream Hollywood cinema. Mulvey insists on the skilled and satisfying manipulation of visual pleasure in Hollywood cinema, especially as it represents women. It is precisely this manipulation—its fixing of women as sexualized objects of the "male gaze"—that Kerkar tries to avoid, especially because in the North African context, male pleasure in looking is easily paired with the colonialist pleasure of looking at the subjugated.

The obsessions of the colonial gaze were concentrated on a single site: the harem. As Malek Alloula has shown in his important book *The Colonial Harem,* in reference to Algerian or Arab women, the simplest allusion to harem initiates a "deployment of phantasm.[4]" In the series of postcards that Alloula analyzed, women appear in two modes—either hidden and veiled or uncovered and exposed—and they are always objectified. The women in these "harem" postcards are never in movement, much less at work. In *Archipel,* Kerkar plays with the imagery of the "colonial harem" by choosing a place—the tannery—that is symbolically opposite to the harem. Kerkar carries certain stereotypes over from the private space of the harem to the public space of the factory, but only to invert their signification. When he films the workers' faces, covered with the masks that protect them from toxic vapors, the viewer sees a clear reference to the *hayek,* a piece of white or beige fabric that women in some regions of North Africa use to cover their faces. Alloula has noted that the veil of Algerian

---

[3] Laura Mulvey, "Visual Pleasure and Narrative Cinema", *Screen*, Volume 16, Issue 3, Autumn 1975, p. 7.

[4] Malek Alloula, *The Colonial Harem*. University of Minnesota Press, 1986, p. 3.

women is often seen as a sort of perfect and generalized mask,[5] but in Kerkar's film, the masks are a work tool, an accessory of empowerment: masking here facilitates women's active labor, rather than signaling passivity. Yes, the mask hides the women's facial features, but for a practical reason. At some points in the film, close-ups allow the audience to guess that the women are smiling at the filmmaker (Fig. 5.1). But in Kerkar's new context, these smiles are not staged by or for a "colonialist gaze"—or even a "male gaze"—the women are constantly active, their bodies continuously moving, accomplishing their routine tasks at the tannery. Kerkar makes sure the tannery workers are treated as subjects with agency, within a space that they have made theirs. There is a sense of empowerment conveyed in this documentary: though it includes not a single spoken word, the camera enacts the filmmaker's willingness to humanize these two women by documenting not only their work but also the breaks they take and the way they sit and playfully move their legs.

The title *Archipel* defines the tannery as an island—but an island nevertheless related to other islands around it. That title illustrates, too, the essence of Kerkar's cinema. Kerkar achieves an immersive experience via the film's wordlessness and its narrow focus on the women and the rooms

Fig. 5.1 A masked tannery worker looking at the camera in *Archipels*

<hr />

[5] Malek Alloula, *The Colonial Harem*, p. 11.

of the tannery. But at the same time, the documentary slowly becomes dreamlike: Kerkar captures the metallic sounds of the machinery, which combine to create a kind of music; the sound of the birds outside the factory; and even the sound of a bird that enters the factory through the window. Some still shots are very poetic: in one scene the insistence of the camera allows the viewer to persist in imagining a barrel full of sticks as a vase of flowers. While filming the women's work, Kerkar also wanted to represent what was transpiring in their minds. It's not surprising that the filmmaker initially considered complementing the images with some verses from the Algerian poet Kateb Yacine but he eventually abandoned that plan, feeling the addition would be intrusive, introducing his own universe in the women's world. Immersion, poetry, and the pursuit of truth through documentary would become the basis upon which Kerkar would go on to structure his first feature documentary film *Atlal*.

ATLAL: A CINEMATOGRAPHIC RESPONSE TO A HISTORIOGRAPHIC IMPASSE

Kerkar said in our interview that he had always hoped to film the Mitidja, a plain that extends along the outskirts of the capital in northern Algeria; the Mitidja has traditionally been devoted to agriculture and serves as the breadbasket of Algiers. The area has in recent decades become increasingly urbanized, as the city of Algiers has expanded. Kerkar chose to film this region—which he routinely visited as child—because it had been hit hard by the Civil War.

I have already explained, in my first chapter, why the representations of the Civil War have always been under the Algerian state scrutiny. A closer look at what happened in the Mitdja is necessary to understand the broader political significance of Kerkar's choice. In the Mitidja, as in many other parts of Algeria, the Islamist party, *Le Front islamique du salut* (FIS) had received a strong majority of the votes in the early 1990s, first in local elections and then in legislative elections. In January 1992, when the army canceled the second round of the legislative elections and declared the FIS illegal, many Islamists fled the important urban centers located along the edges of the Mitidja—Algiers, Blida, Tipaza, Boumerdès, and Médea and settled in the mountains situated in the south of the region. There they formed paramilitary movements for initiating a *jihad* against the military-controlled state. Some zones were the witness of daily combats and clashes.[6]

Faced with a situation that was getting steadily violent, the regime embarked in 1993 on a military campaign, striving to reassert control over the Islamist communes of Greater Algiers and the Mitidja. In a parallel action, the national government implemented a policy of terror, here directed against the people of Algeria, whom the regime hoped to dissuade from supporting the groups committed to armed struggle against the state. Practices of torture, humiliation, and deadly reprisals carried out by the security forces provoked an outburst of violence in the communes of the Mitidja.[7] Civilians were massacred by the hundreds, particularly during 1997, when mass killings took place in the villages of Raïs and Betalha. These massacres, claimed by terrorist organizations, raised doubts among many regarding the real identity of the perpetrators: were the terrorists acting alone, or were they being manipulated by the secret services? As francophone and international media (over)simplified the situation: *qui tue qui?* or "who kills whom?" This complicated question remains controversial in Algeria, as it contains the possibility that the military secret services may bear or share responsibility for the violence of the 1990s. Because of the undisputed atrocities its people suffered, and because of that still-disputed responsibility, the Mitidja epitomizes the complexities of a "dirty war" that shook the nation, the ramifications of which have not yet been fully examined in the public arena.[8]

By choosing to film the Mitidja, Djamel Kerkar wanted to capture how the region still bore the memory of this profound trauma, even as the signs and symptoms of the trauma were slowly disappearing. After some scouting in the region, Kerkar decided to film the village of Ouled Allal that was almost destroyed during the 1990s conflict. The inhabitants were forced to move to safer regions and some villagers had returned in the 2000s. The choice of location made it inevitable that Kerkar's

---

[6] Luis Martinez, *La guerre civile en Algérie*. Éditions Karthala, 1998, p. 101.

[7] Luis Martinez, *La guerre civile en Algérie*, p. 22.

[8] Some first-person accounts have reinforced the hypothesis that the secret service(s) may have played a role in the conflict. These accounts, written by former members of the military secret service or the Algerian Army and published in France include most notably Nesroulah Yous, *Qui a tué à Bentalha? Algérie: chronique d'un massacre annoncé*. La découverte, 2000; Habib Souaïdia, *La sale guerre. Le témoignage d'un ancien officier des forces spéciales de l'armée algérienne*. La Découverte, 2012; Aboud, Hichem, *La Mafia des Généraux*. JC Lattès, 2002.

documentary would talk about the Civil War; recognizing that the film-maker's approach to the topic could potentially upset or contradict the official narrative, his producer Jaber Debzi opted not to apply to the Algerian minister of culture for permissions, lest he risk a prison sentence for "endangering public order" or threatening "national unity."

Atlal can be understood as Kerkar's cinematographic response to a his-toriographic impasse. The film aims to make seen and heard what the state has rendered invisible and silent. It shows the restorative power of a docu-mentary that explores the past and the present—and consciously distances itself from any pre-constructed discourse about the Civil War. Nevertheless, despite the film's necessary focus on destruction and loss, Kerkar tries to find glimpses of light and hope.

As Djamel Kerkar himself points out during our conversations, Ouled Allal is not a *lieu de mémoire*,[9] it is not a place of remembrance marked by monuments, commemorative plaques, or museums dedicated to impor-tant past events. Instead, Kerkar films Ouled Allal as a place where mem-ory can unfold, where the spectator anticipates an as-yet-unrevealed tragic memory. The geography of the village is therefore very important to the film; Kerkar uses its layout to structure the process of recovering a lost narrative about the Civil War. The village is in fact divided into two seg-ments: the first one is inhabited by villagers who try to keep up with their daily lives and rebuild the place; the second segment is composed of ruins, attesting to the destruction of the Civil War. Yet the new village under construction and the abandoned ruins often look alike—Kerkar's camera repeatedly juxtaposes the construction sites of the emerging new village against the debris of the ruins.

In making the documentary, Kerkar has chosen to ignore the official archives completely. He never superposes the memories of the inhabitants and the official records of the state, and never explicitly attempts to expose the differences between them. Instead, he relies exclusively on "unofficial sources"—especially recorded testimonies of the least authoritative social subjects—and incorporates a variety of other records gathered from diverse sources—home-movies, photographs. Nature and geography serve a fur-ther documentary role, as Kerkar captures the marks and scars inscribed upon the landscapes in and around Ouled Allal.

---

[9] Djamel Kerkar borrows the expression from Pierre Nora, who, in his influential book *Les lieux de mémoire,* explores sites that participate in generating French history and memory, See Pierre Nora, *Les lieux de mémoire.* Quarto Gallimard, 1997, p. 29.

To gather and combine his unofficial "documents," Kerkar used an immersive approach. For a month he went daily to the village with his camera, filming places such as gardens or houses and taking pictures. People who started noticing his presence began to ask him which media outlet he worked for. Abdou—at age 17 one of the documentary's youngest characters—mentions that representatives of these official channels came occasionally to the village, but he says their work was superficial and the results didn't really capture the village's daily struggles. As we saw in Chap. 4 regarding Ferhani's documentaries *Dans ma tête un rond-point* and *143 rue du desert*, many Algerians voice suspicion regarding national media that they associate with the stories the government wants told. In the village, day after day, as he met inhabitants from different neighborhoods, from multiple generations, Kerkar had to patiently explain his project, stressing his independence from the state.

Shooting the documentary took three months. Kerkar spent a full month in the village in the fall of 2016, during which he mostly filmed landscapes and buildings and talked with the residents without filming them. Several weeks later he returned to spend two additional months on location, filming the inhabitants as they told their stories. It is through his long work of observation and immersion, as well as his openness to unofficial sources, that Kerkar was able to find the archival images that he has eventually used to open the film. The documentary begins with 14 minutes of VHS images, slightly blurred and unstable, images filmed in 1998, in Ouled Allal. Kerkar learned about this old video footage during a conversation with a villager who explained that an architect had spent time in Ouled Allal, in 1998, and had filmed the village, after fights between military and Islamists. Because Kerkar had, by this time, built close relationships in the village, he was able to locate the man who guided the architect in 1998. His contacts were pessimistic, warning Kerkar that the owner of the footage could not even be brought to talk about the period of the Civil War. In the end, after many conversations, the villager trusted Kerkar enough that he not only allowed him to view the images but ultimately gave him a copy on CD, with permission to use the images in his film.

These grainy 1998 VHS images are thus the first testimony the movie offers to the audience. That Kerkar has used them to open the film conveys from the very beginning the filmmaker's documentary ethic: he wants to return to images that haven't been used in the media in a "*reportage*" mode and to document the past, removed from any pre-constructed discourse about the Civil War. The images filmed by the architect and the villager who led him through Ouled Allal are powerful. They show run-down buildings and a deadly landscape that combine to express the horror of what people went through. They convey a genuine sense of chaos and let the audience gradually realize the amplitude of the catastrophe that the village has experienced. The date is not mentioned at first but appears after three minutes of decontextualized images, when a time stamp shows up at the bottom left of the screen: "October 19, 1998, 11:04 AM." The view-er's perception of chaos is emphasized by the sound, as the wind saturates the soundtrack. The first image is of a single farmer's boot. The spectator is invited to imagine how people left the village in a hurry, leaving nearly everything behind. The camera continues, zooming in on abandoned objects: chairs, machines, fences. Everything is in ruins: destroyed houses falling apart, a debris of walls, balconies and rooves, exposed steel bars that would usually be buried deep within the remaining walls they sustain. During the 14 minutes, the audience hears only wind and silence. Human voices are introduced just twice, and only for a few seconds at a time. We hear the architect who is filming ask where they are, and the villager answers, "The village … Ouled Allal." Later the same villager says, "The village is as big as Azrine." Azrine is the angel of death in the Islamic tradi-tion, and the comparison signals the scale of disaster the VHS camera relentlessly records.

At the 14-minute mark, the film's transition from the archival images to the present insists on the deep connection between archival past and pres-ent: the archival images conclude with a blue screen and give way to the blue of the sky that Kerkar films 20 years later, at the same place, with the same ruins. These archival images do, in fact, contain numerous signs that explicitly reference the catastrophe that has so recently occurred. Kerkar includes an image of a graffiti tag with the acronym "FIS" for the Islamist party, *Le Front islamique du salut*, a reminder that region had in fact voted for the Islamist party candidate in the 1991 parliamentary elections. These archival images create a system of indexicality within Kerkar's documen-tary itself. Indexical images from the 1990s are echoed within Kerkar's images. A water tower that first appears in the archival images of 1998 functions as a key indexical image. In the archival footage, the architect zooms in first on a hole in a wall and only gradually does the audience realize he is filming a water tower. The same tower will appear several times in Kerkar's images but as a more discreet sign, usually in the back-ground. The tower once appears fleetingly in a photograph that belongs to *'ammi* Rabah (Uncle Rabah),[10] the oldest character in Kerkar's documentary. The visual echoes of the water tower throughout the film help the spectator realize the complex links between past and present, film and memory.

Writing about memory films, David Macdougall has distinguished different ways that signs are employed in film, differentiating between signs of replacement and signs of resemblance.[11] When a documentary tries to translate a memory, a filmmaker will usually use signs of *replacement* to communicate to the viewer that an object or an archive—be it a picture or a film or a home movie—is the memory itself. Music in memory films, on the other hand, is a sign of *resemblance*, because music is directly related to emotion and also because music can condition the audience to regard the past with a certain degree of melancholy, nostalgia, or fear.[12] Kerkar doesn't use music during his film, except for music that his protagonists listened to or sing.

Kerkar could have used the archival footage to illustrate some of the testimony he collects in his film, but he chose not to do so. Instead of weaving the archival images throughout the film or using them as an illustration of memories retold by the characters in the documentary and invoking them as signs of replacement, Kerkar's project was to explore the site to the best of his ability, not in the classic investigative mode of the journalist, but rather by filming again the same location, allowing the village to tell its own story through landscapes, ruins, new buildings, and the testimonies of its inhabitants. Some memory films lead the audience to believe that the past can be retrieved, as if films can state a true version of facts. There is, in this process, a risk of elegy, an implication that the memories of the characters are intrinsically virtuous. An elegiac recovery of the past is not what Kerkar tries to achieve with *Atlal*. He does not hide the voids and blanks in a character's memory but wants instead to convey the process of memory with its echoes, its holes, its incoherence, its strange mixture of verbal and sensorial elements—and also its mental landscapes.

Three generations of villagers appear in the documentary. Each generation lives in a different location, and each experienced the Civil War

---

[10] In All the names mentionned in this documentary *'ammi* means uncle and is a sign of respect.

[11] David Macdougall, "Films de mémoire," *Journal des anthropologues*, n°47-48, Printemps 1992.

[12] David Macdougall, "Films de mémoire," p. 72.

differently. *'Ammi* Rabah is the oldest character, and the story of his life echoes the story of Algeria from the period of colonization, through the Civil War, to the present of narration. He has been a farm worker all his life and has a strong attachment to the land as he describes it in a very moving scene, crying when evoking how long he worked the same piece of land. Three middle-aged men who witnessed closely the events of the Civil War, compose the second generational group. Lakhdar lives in dire conditions far away from his children, and in speaking to Kerkar, he reveals a traumatic part of his life during the Civil War. Ahmed, Meriem's father, is building a new house with his own two hands. Kerkar doesn't film him telling his story, but mainly captures him while working on the house. There is, finally, *'ammi* Lakhdar, the current imam of the village, who narrates his memories in two different scenes. In the first, he is alone, working on his tree plantation; in the second, he is in the streets, and younger men surround him while he talks about events that happened during the conflict. The third generation is composed of young men who were too young at the time to fully understand what was going and thus have scattered memories of the 1990's conflict. Abdou, the youngest protagonist of the film, is a high school student who hangs out with his friends in the reconstructed part of the village. He is the character who introduces an important shift in the film because Kerkar was able to film him and his friends at night, while the documentary's other characters appear only in daylight.

As Kerkar described it during our conversation, the documentary required spending hours at a time with all these men—without filming them—to establish an atmosphere of trust and complicity. This, he hoped, would allow him to avoid the stereotyped conversations they might have enacted in front of TV cameras. The goal of establishing trust also explains why Kerkar let each character choose the site where he wanted to be filmed when telling his story. The geographical divide appears clearly between the three generations. The oldest men return far more frequently to places that bear the marks and traces of the Civil War, while Abdou and his friends stay away from the ruins (with one exception in the film, as we will see below).

Kerkar films many characters, but only four share what can be described as testimonies[13]: *'Ammi* Rabah, *'ammi* Lakhdar, Lakhdar, and Abdou.

---

[13] Contrary to other countries like Argentina that have experienced modern political trauma, Algeria has not seen the development of a testimonial genre with its centering of first-person witnessing and its implied factuality.

Their stories unfold before the camera in first-person accounts that nevertheless center on a problematic collective situation that the narrators undergo alongside others. Testimonial narrative in the aftermath of a traumatic event like a civil war, entails an experience of mourning, which is necessarily subjective and private. In telling their stories, the characters situate themselves in the vulnerable space between the "impossibility of telling" and the necessity of telling as a step toward healing.[14] To be fully understood, their accounts must be contextualized and Kerkar, rather than add an explicit voiceover, instead silently offers as the context the geography of Ouled Allal itself. The landscapes Kerkar features abundantly throughout transitional shots, and the terrain and buildings and ruins that form the backgrounds for his characters' observations and memories, function as a geographical incarnation of the speakers' mental reality. They also bear witness to what happened and often complete the blanks and holes of stories too difficult to tell.

The first character to speak in the documentary after twenty long minutes of near silence is *'ammi* Lakhdar. The spectator first sees him working—for several minutes we watch him gathering dead trees and branches. He then describes the farm around him and tells its story. He speaks of the trees that were planted in 1991, just before the Civil War began. He is very precise and provides exact numbers—700 apple trees and 1300 peach trees—and the audience trusts him as someone who knows the orchards well. When the inhabitants fled the area, because of the violence that was happening in and around the village, they left everything behind. When they returned in 2002, *'ammi* Lakhdar says they found the trees in a complete state of shock: *mchokyin*, all of them destroyed. This personification of the trees is a way to communicate via the wounded trees, what likewise happened to the people of the village; *'ammi* Lakhdar describes trauma for exactly what it is, a shock caused by a sudden stimulus for which the organism has no opportunity to prepare.

Since the 1990s, trauma theory has developed as an important framework for interpreting and understanding testimonial narratives. Cathy Caruth defines trauma as "an overwhelming experience of sudden or catastrophic events in which the response to these events occurs in the often

---

[14] Shoshana Felman and Dori Laub, *Testimony: Crises of Witnessing in Literature, Psychoanalysis, and History*. Routledge, 1991, p. 79.

delayed and uncontrolled appearance of intrusive phenomena."[15] Trauma, as Caruth observes, is more than a pathology: it is also the voice of a past truth that cries out and remains otherwise unavailable. When 'ammi Lakhdar looks into the camera, the audience can see his pain as mention of the past recalls the emotions felt during the period of the civil war.

Collecting testimonies is at once "historical and clinical...a medium of historical transmission and the unsuspected medium of healing."[16] Kerkar is aware of this responsibility, and he mentioned in his interviews with me that it took him some time to set up his conversation with the oldest character of the film, 'ammi Rabah, whom Kerkar thought was very fragile. Like the previous character, 'ammi Rabah chose to be filmed on agricultural land, sitting beside a tree. The location in effect tells his story, as he explains that he spent all his life working as a farmer. European farmers had hired him during colonization; after the country's independence, when the lands were nationalized by the Algerian state, he continued to work the same fields. His sense of belonging to the land is clear when he explains how, during the Civil War, he had to defend the village and protect it again, this time from Islamist terrorists. He becomes overwhelmed by his emotions and begins to weep.

Because of his age and his long experience, 'ammi Rabah effectively constitutes the memory of the village. And it is likely because of his capacity to represent this geographical memory that Kerkar's contextualization of 'ammi Rabah's trauma is made through landscape and through the photographs that this lifelong agricultural laborer has brought with him to the filming site. This encounter with 'ammi Rabah is thus the second time that Kerkar uses personal archives in the film, and the viewer can compare these photographs to the archival images of the film's opening, recognizing that the photographs 'ammi Rabah offers up to the camera reiterate the story in the early VHS clip. Kerkar films the photographs as 'ammi Rabah shares his story, but he does so without trying to zoom in or capture every detail of each photograph. 'Ammi Rabah's spoken memories allows for a recuperation of the past in which the testimonial narrative and the personal archives don't have to tell anything other than what 'ammi Rabah wants them to say. Kerkar is intentionally reversing the traditional process of memory films that use archival visual material to complement

---

[15] Cathy Caruth, *Unclaimed experience: trauma, Narrative, and History.* Johns Hopkins University Press, 1996, p. 11.

[16] Shoshana Felman and Dori Laub, *Testimony*, p. 9.

the stories heard on screen. *Atlal* becomes itself an alternative archive but without mimicking the rigor or precision of an official one.

Because trauma can sometimes stifle the capacity to voice a description of what happened, it is not unusual for survivors of trauma to report that memories reemerge when they are least expected. This happens once during the film, when Kerkar is filming Lakhdar who appears several times in the film, playing with a street dog, but saying little. One evening, Lakhdar joins Abdou and his friends and sits with them around a bonfire. They share stories and anecdotes while listening to rap and raï music on their phones. For Lakhdar, the cold and the fire bring back old memories of his military service during the Civil War. Lakhdar begins by retrieving a fairly innocuous memory of being stationed in the region of Médéa, which is known for its cold winters. He remembers with a laugh that he had to wear several layers of clothes, and he remembers once having to drain the water from a car radiator so it wouldn't freeze. After this light anecdote, his friends want to change the subject. They tell Lakhdar he must forget this period of his life, but he abruptly answers, "I can't forget it." They indulge him by asking if he was shot. His answer is striking: "The bullets, they are nothing, I survived them. I almost lost my mind there!" Lakhdar tells his listeners that he was among the first of his regiment to arrive in Berouaguia after the first time the city was attacked by Islamist terrorists. He describes the events as a "massacre"; he reveals a moment when he found the body of a seven-month-old baby, dead and cut into pieces. He says he couldn't sleep for weeks, that the image of this baby haunted him for a long time. He then stays silent, listening to a song of singer Chab Hasni, a raï singer who was assassinated in 1994 by an Islamist group. Lakhdar is the character who seems most impacted by the Civil War, and that is probably the reason Kerkar gave him the last words of the documentary, signaling that it will take more than participating in a documentary, or offering a brief testimony of his traumatic experience, to deliver healing.

The youngest character of the film, Abdou, seems at first glance to have only a vague memory of what happened during the Civil War—a lack of specificity that sets him apart from the other characters. He seems more concerned with the present. He speaks at length about love, unemployment, and lack of opportunities for young people like him, and he posits emigration as the only solution that can give him a chance to live a decent life. In his interview with me, Kerkar said that he had a different relationship to this character because of his young age. The filmmaker doesn't hesitate to challenge Abdou and pushes back gently on Abdou's hopes of traveling clandestinely to Europe, reminding him that this is not an easy journey to complete. But over the course of their conversations, as we had seen in Kerkar's interactions with Lakhdar, Abdou reveals important information about his life. He mentions that he has often asked his mother why she had a child during the "terrorism," knowing that he would grow up surrounded by violence and rifle bullets. He adds that his father died during the Civil War. This was a traumatic event for Abdou, but the details also engage a great taboo in the public memory of the Civil War: his father's body was never recovered, and thus Abdou cannot say if he was killed by Islamists or by the military or by other State forces. His father was taken from his home, and what happened to him after that remains a mystery.

When telling his father's story, Abdou provocatively refuses the official distinction between terrorists and the state with a simple sentence: "Isn't the State (*dawla*) acting like terrorists when you see what they do to us?" In so doing, he questions the entire official narrative of the Algerian regime, whose new legitimacy rests on its claim to have saved Algeria from Islamist terrorist forces. It does not really matter if Abdou's analysis of the past is accurate: what matters is that with his father's story he contests the official narrative of reconciliation and peace that the regime has imposed. With his pointed comment about terrorism, and his determination to tell his father's story, he implicitly hints at other untold stories. We see in real time, then, Kerkar realizing his goal: not to show what "truly" happened, but to allow people to simply tell their stories. Peacemaking is often speculative and there is no right or wrong model, but Algeria's efforts toward peace and reconciliation are a major departure from what is often called the "truth model" of reconciliation, illustrated by South Africa's post-apartheid "Truth and Reconciliation Commission.[17]" Some historians have used the term "state-sponsored amnesia" to describe the policy that discouraged public and collective re-elaboration of the traumatic past of the Lebanese Civil Wars; and even if the contexts are slightly different the expression also applies to Algeria in the 2000s.[18] *Atlal* can be seen as a call to further restorative justice, a larger process that would allow narratives and memories to unfold and counterbalance what the Algerian regime has

---

[17] James, D. Le Sueur, *Algeria since 1989: between Terror and democracy*. Zed Books, 2010, p. 80.

[18] Elisa Adami, "The Truth of Fiction: Some Stories of the Lebanese Civil Wars", in Karine Deslandes, Fabrice Mourlon and Bruno Tribout (ed.), *Civil War and Narrative. Testimony. Historiography, Memory*. Palgrave Macmillan, 2017.

tried to do by quickly turning the page and by striving in the ensuing years to control any discourse about the conflict.

In Kerkar's film, the nature of the discourse has probably as much to do with poetry as it does with restorative testimonies. The title of the film itself references a specific genre in ancient Arabic poetry, an *atlal* is indeed a four-verse poem that a poet declaims while standing in front of ruins. As we have seen above, the village of Ouled Allal was ravaged by war. As the VHS camera waits before the village's ruins in the 1998 footage, there is at first only silence—or, at least, there are no words. The spectator can only hear the wind and the varied sounds of the village's daily life: construction, car honks, etc. This silence serves multiple functions. It first conveys trauma as it typically experienced through silence, and the incapability of finding the proper words to describe the wounds inflicted. At the figurative level, we can also experience the opening minutes of silence as that imposed on Algerians after the Civil Concord of 1999, as article 45 of that concord denied victims the opportunity to press charges or even to talk about their experiences after terrorists and certain Islamist leaders had been pardoned. And yet neither the silence of trauma nor the silence imposed by the State prevents Kerkar from looking for words, and even for bursts of poetry and hope.

Kerkar, in our interview, recalled being deeply moved by the scene in the archival images where the architect is filming the blasted water tower. The architect ends the scene by trying to capture something on the floor: eventually the spectator realizes that he is filming flowers that have managed to grow amid chaos. This scene resonated deeply with Kerkar: he recalls that he saw it as a desperate longing for poetry in the middle of so much destruction. But the character in the film who would logically be considered a poet is Abdou. Like a young Baudelaire he smokes cannabis and patiently prepares his joints directly in front of Kerkar's camera, unafraid of what might happen to him (smoking cannabis is illegal in Algeria and can be punished with time in prison). Sitting among the ruins, he writes down the lyrics of a rap song and then reads them to Kerkar. In a beautiful scene, as the moon rises behind Abdou against a purple-blue sky, he invokes the moon to explain how he feels about the Algerian state: he would rather be cut off suddenly from oxygen—a bomb explodes, and he lands on the moon—than continue in the slow suffocation where the Algerian state gradually takes away the air he needs to breathe. Here the exploding bomb is not an image of the traumatic events of the Civil War; for Abdou, in this moment, it is a tool that—in a variation on his emigration dreams—could bring him to a place of freedom.

The filmmaker himself acts as a poet, standing before the ruins with his camera, exploring the landscapes and the memories of Ouled Allal's inhabitants. Into this film—a project Kerkar has said he considered urgent—he brings images of a constellation of beings, voices, bodies, and buildings that all have faced the test of time. By filming a place that he used to know as a child, he takes a political and poetic stance, slowly showing emotions, unfolding his characters' speeches, and liberating words. His documentary thus gradually outlines different histories and builds a new narrative about contemporary Algeria.

Despite difficult and unstable circumstances, the country's construction is ongoing and still hints at the possibility of more work to come. Ahmed is undoubtedly the character whose presence instills hope. Not only is he building his own house, but he is doing the work himself; it is very moving to see his daughter Meriem keeping him company as he works on the house. One incredibly beautiful scene summarizes this paradoxical idea of hopeful instability. As Kerkar explained during my interview with him, Ahmed one day discovered that someone had borrowed his ladder when he needed it. Instead of asking for it to be returned, Ahmed tried to work with what he could find: we thus see him in a beautifully framed shot, standing on a barrel, piled bricks, and a wooden board, and reaching toward a window (Fig. 5.2). His balance is precarious—he

Fig. 5.2 Meriem's father building his house, standing precariously on a chair *in Atlal*

seems on the verge of falling—but somehow, he manages to stay on his feet and to keep on working, metaphorically representing every Algerian citizen trying to cope with the lingering trauma of the Civil War, making do with limited resources, and working to rebuild the present to ensure the future.

References

Aboud, Hichem. *La Mafia des Généraux*. Paris: JC Lattès, 2002

Alloula, Malek. *The Colonial Harem*. Minneapolis: University of Minnesota Press, 1986.

Brahimi, Denise. *Regards sur les cinémas du Maghreb*. Paris: Éditions Petra, 2016.

Caruth, Cathy. *Unclaimed experience: trauma, narrative, and history*. Baltimore: Johns Hopkins University Press, 1996.

Denis, Sébastien. *Le Cinéma et la guerre d'Algérie: la propagande à l'écran (1945-1962)*. Paris: Nouveau Monde éditions, 2009.

Deslandes, Karine and Fabrice Mourlon and Bruno Tribout (ed.), *Civil War and Narrative. Testimony. Historiography, Memory*. Cham, Switzerland: Palgrave Macmillan, 2017.

Felman, Shoshana and Dori Laub, *Testimony: Crises of Witnessing in Lliterature, Psychoanalysis, and History*. Routledge, 1991.

Le Sueur, James D. *Between terror and democracy: Algeria since 1989*. London New York: Zed Book, 2010.

Macdougall, David. "Films de mémoire," *Journal des anthropologues*, n°47–48, Spring, 1992.

Martinez, Luis. *La guerre civile en Algérie*. Éditions Karthala, 1998.

Mulvey, Laura. "Visual Pleasure and Narrative Cinema", *Screen*, Volume 16, Issue 3, Autumn 1975.

Nora, Pierre. *Les lieux de mémoire*, Paris: Quarto Gallimard, 1997.

Souaïdia, Habib. *La sale guerre. Le témoignage d'un ancien officier des forces spéciales de l'armée algérienne*, Paris, La Découverte, 2012.

Yous, Nesroulah. *Qui a tué à Bentalha? Algérie: chronique d'un massacre annoncé*. Paris: La découverte, 2000.

CHAPTER 6

Karim Sayad: Disrupting Myths of Masculinity

> *It's dawn and sleep won't come.*
> *I'm consuming in small doses.*
> *Why? Who should I blame?*
> *We're sick of this life.—Ouled El Bahdja*

Karim Sayad's three documentaries—*Babor Casanova* (2015), *Des moutons et des hommes* (2017), and *My English Cousin* (2019)—follow male subjects, exclusively in the first two films and primarily in the third. From football team fans to competitors in clandestine sheep fights and finally to his cousin, an illegal immigrant who manages to build a life in Great Britain, the men Sayad films belong to a part of the population that is often talked about in the media but whose members are rarely offered a chance to speak for themselves. Sayad is responding to generalized representations in popular culture and media that describe a monolithic Algerian masculinity often and too quickly called *radjla*.[1] But *radjla*—which is the popular version of the classic Arabic word *moroua*—does not connote virility or toxic masculinity as it is often construed, but rather a more

---

[1] *Radjla* is the implicit missing term in the title of one of the most important Algerian movies about masculinity, *Omar Gatlato* (1977). The title translates as "Omar was killed." And everyone in Algeria knows the missing words here are "by *radjla*."

© The Author(s), under exclusive license to Springer Nature Switzerland AG 2023
M. Belkaïd, *From Outlaw to Rebel*, Palgrave Studies in Arab Cinema, https://doi.org/10.1007/978-3-031-19157-2_6

chivalrous ethos. It has even a sense of "masculine modesty" that implies self-respect and extreme decency toward others.

As for representation of manhood, the majority of scholarship dealing with gender issues in Algerian cinema focuses on female rather than male identity. Few scholars have analyzed representations of masculinity in Algerian fiction. Andrea Khalil has brilliantly studied how filmmaker Merzak Allouache questions some myths of masculinity throughout his fictional feature films. Khalil begins from the concept of mythology as defined by Roland Barthes rather than engaging with hegemonic masculinity per se, arguing that Allouache's male characters question preconceived idea about masculinity by showing vulnerability and even homosexual tendencies.[2] More recently, Mani Sharpe in an article about representations of masculinity in postcolonial Algerian cinema discusses a critical blind spot, showing that men are not systematically represented as fearless warriors and martyrs, even in films sponsored by the state and aligned with nationalist hegemonic discourse.[3]

In his films, Sayad questions preconceived negative notions about the malevolence of Algerian men because of a narrow understanding of *radjla*. He allows his characters to express their thoughts, dreams, and regrets. He creates a safe space of camaraderie where they feel comfortable enough to share challenges they face and most of all their vulnerability and their contradictions. He reframes the stereotypical representations of the men of the region, breaking the narrative of toxic masculinity and violence and offering portraits of vulnerability, fragility, and ambivalence. His documentaries thus foreshadow what we've seen in Algeria since February 2019, when news media were astonished by the pacifist nature of the social movement and suddenly discovered the important role that young male soccer fans assumed in the early days of the protest.

Sayad's documentaries question what we think we know about Algerian men as patriarchs, polygamists, violent protestors, religious fanatics, and terrorists. His films work as antidotes to these stereotypes as, through immersion, he humanizes men who have been categorically condemned in media and cultural perception, especially since the Algerian Civil War and

---

[2] Andrea Khalil, "The Myth of Masculinity in the Films of Merzak Allouache," *Journal of North African Studies* 12, no.3, 2007.

[3] Mani Sharpe, "Representing Masculinity in Postcolonial Algerian Cinema," *Journal of North African Studies* 20, no. 3, 2015.

more broadly since 9/11. [4] Sayad's films offer a variety of portraits, and he uses cross-cutting editing techniques to significant effect, allowing the spectator to understand masculinities as plural and diverse, locally situated, and historically contingent.

HUMANIZING SOCCER FANS

Sayad's first documentary follows two young men who are supporters of one of Algiers's soccer teams, *Le Mouloudia Club d'Alger*. Djemil Adlan Cherif, 19 years old, spends his days waiting for his team's weekend games. The documentary never mentions his best friend's name and age; the spectator knows him only through his nickname *Irhabi* ("terrorist"). Both are unemployed, both dream of living abroad, taking the imaginary boat of the documentary's title *Babor Casanova*. This boat is mentioned in the lyrics of a song in praise of their beloved team. The documentary also shows the two young men smoking hashish and considering buying a small bottle of a detergent that is used as an inhalant.

Djemil and Irahibi's unemployment renders them nearly indescribable in social terms. To get the money they need for soccer game tickets and for traveling to other cities to watch their team, they work as *parkingueurs*, an Algerian neologism pairing parking with the professional suffix -eur. In these informal jobs, young men get paid for helping drivers park their cars in improvised parking spaces and then watching the cars until their owners return.

In many neighborhoods of the capital, traffic is dense and parking spots very rare. Young men in Algiers engage in this unofficial activity, creating some tension between the *parkingueurs* and drivers who often see them as racketeers. The young *parkingueurs* respond to wary drivers by trying to assert their authority and legitimize, if not actually impose, their business. The physical setting (the street) and the situation (asserting oneself) sets the stage for these young men to enact a version of hegemonic masculinity as "performative acts." [5] In one documentary sequence, for instance, when we see Djemil reluctantly dismiss a driver who refuses to pay him,

---

[4] See, for example, for a stereotypical representation of Algerian men, Andrew Hussey, *The French Intifada: The Long War Between France and Its Arabs*. Granta, 2014.

[5] Judith Butler, "Performative Acts and Gender Constitution: An Essay in Phenomenology and Feminist Theory", *Theatre Journal*, Dec., 1988, Vol. 40, No. 4 (Dec., 1988), pp. 519-531

Djemil is at least partly engaged in a performance of masculinity. The spectator understands the driver's repeated claims that he doesn't have any change. And Djemil is, in turn, aware of the camera's presence: he looks at the camera, conscious that he is being filmed. Viewers of any documentary know that the camera, even in an immersive situation, introduces the idea of performance or even sometimes of "mise en scène."[6] Nevertheless, what is interesting here is to see firsthand Djemil's negotiation with the camera and with his own beliefs about virility and masculinity.

Later in the documentary, Sayad includes another scene in which Djemil tells the story of an altercation with another driver who refused to pay. First Djemil took the driver's hat, and then his friend stunned the driver with a Taser. The police arrived a few minutes later, and Djemil had to spend 20 days in jail. This account—whether true or false—works as a counterpoint to the events of the scene mentioned above. Here Djemil tells a story in which he didn't let the driver go as easily and was able to assert his power over the driver directly with the help of a friend. The story shows that if Djemil didn't perform violent behavior in front of the camera at the time, he nevertheless sees this mention of violence as important to conforming with a certain idea of masculinity. Djemil, via his narrative, performs the violence he previously withheld.

In their social and familial marginalization and their apparent isolation—and probably also because of their young age—Djemil and Irhabi betray difficulty in displaying what would be considered as "successful manhood." The soccer club plays the role of socializer, creating purpose and community and, to some extent, a new manhood or what Marcia C. Inhorn terms, an "emergent masculinity."[7] Stadiums and mosques are important male spaces in Algeria; they are generally considered the only options for young men to socialize. These spaces are symbolically opposed in the sense that a young man's choice is either to become a football supporter, which would likely make of him a "bad boy," or to become a regular visitor of the mosque, which would identify him as an "Islamist" or even a "fanatic." These perceptions are reflected in state communications that would divide the nation's youth into two groups, each individually threatening to the state's power and stability but perceived as less dangerous divided than united. With one simple scene, Sayad questions this

---

[6] François Niney, *Le documentaire et ses faux-semblants*. Klincksieck, 2009.

[7] Marcia C. Inhorn, *The New Arab Man. Emergent Masculinities, Technologies, and Islam in the Middle East*. Princeton University Press, 2012.

divide: he shows young men praying while at the stadium, using the team's flags as prayer rugs. Sayad poignantly questions our assumptions, suggesting greater social complexity and undermining the constructed barrier between perceived sports fanatic and religious fanatic.

It is interesting, then, to question the nickname "Irhabi" used by Djemil's friend. The word clearly refers to the Algerian Civil War or to other, more recent, manifestations of terrorism in Algeria. Although the Islamist civil conflict has quieted in the 2000s, Islamist extremism remains present in Algeria under Al Qaeda in the Islamic Maghreb (AQIM), a branch of Al Qaeda that grew out of the Algerian Islamist extremist groups that fought in the 1990s Civil War. The Civil War of the 1990s and subsequent, if sporadic, political violence amount to what Raewyn Connell calls a historical trauma, one that has the capacity to "provoke attempts to restore a dominant masculinity" perceived as impaired by the damages of war and economic uncertainty. [8] Connell sees violence in tumultuous times as a way that men can assert masculinity in group struggles because when violence takes the shape of terror, it draws boundaries and makes exclusions. In times of terror, men are encouraged to enforce masculine norms by monitoring the behaviors of other men. During the Civil War, terrorists positioned their political violence at the center of an idealized Algerian society that would be free from both French colonial influence and from local forms of political corruption. These militarized men provided new social codes to which everyone was expected to adhere, and the militarized groups ensured that the codes were enforced through violence.

It is, then, not surprising that the individual man's relationship with this constructed masculinity is ambivalent, oscillating between rejection and fascination. The ironic connotation of the nickname Irhabi would not be lost on contemporary Algerian viewers. The young man is clearly too young to have taken part in the Civil War, and he is not in any way involved in a modern terrorist group. The nickname reveals that young Algerian men know the stereotypes attached to them. By claiming the "insult" as many other dominated groups have done before them—albeit in slightly different political and cultural contexts—Irahabi and his friends highlight popular stereotypes of young men and at the same time they reject the stereotype as ironic. Sayad heightens the tension around Irhabi's nickname via his editing choices: he never resolves the uncertainty by having the character introduce himself, as Djemil does at the beginning of the

---

[8] Raewyn Connell, *Masculinities*. University of California Press, 2005.

documentary, by stating his name, age, and professional status. Irhabi closes the documentary with a poetic gesture: he is hanging onto the back of a van, lying on the vehicle's bumper in the posture of a man enjoying the sun, relaxing in a beach chair. Sayad points out by this cinematographic choice that this moment of release is probably what these young men long for, their share of happiness and contentment.

Sayad's main concern in *Babor Casanova* is to question the stereotype of the young fan as thug, demonstrating that their passion for the football team transcends simple obsession and works as a socializer that grounds them, gives them purpose, and allows them to inhabit a version of manhood that, if it does not correspond to the hegemonic masculine stereotype, does afford them a sense of agency. The stadiums work as a metonymic place and compensate for an anomic society and political arena. The stadium replaces the social field as a whole and becomes the space where everything can be expressed: feelings and emotions, political beliefs, hopes and demands. The depth and the beauty of some football songs cannot be emphasized enough:

> Why do I always feel alone
> Strange and foreign
> Praising God and waiting.

The scenes of the documentary shot in the stadiums are impressive, framing the fans' precisely orchestrated singing, where one section of the stadium answers back to the other. Sayad's aestheticized scenes communicate that the fervor is not only about sports but is also the emotional distress of an entire younger generation that is seeking space for expression.

FAILED MANHOOD VERSUS SUCCESSFUL MANHOOD?

In his 2017 documentary *Des moutons et des hommes*, Sayad goes further in commenting on Algerian myths of masculinity, this time choosing to situate two paradigms of masculinity in apparent opposition. While Djemil and Irhabi displayed many characteristics in common (age, social status, and habits), here the central characters Habib and Samir couldn't be more different from each other. In *Des moutons et des hommes*, Sayad again explores a very masculine setting: Algiers' clandestine sheep fights. The camera follows Samir and Habib, who are deeply involved in this world, the first as a sheep seller and the second as the new owner of a fighting sheep. Samir is 46 years old, lives in the neighborhood of Bab El Oued, and regularly goes into the southern part of the country to buy sheep and resell them for use in fights. He also sells sheep for the sacred holy day of Eid. Habib is a young man who quit school and works as a bus *receveur* (controller); he has saved his earnings and recently acquired a sheep called El Bouq, whom he hopes can win some fights. Sayad's choice of characters opposes not only two generations but what seems, at first glance, to be two different masculinities. In fact, both characters are striving to match their lives against certain masculine attributes, with neither of them always succeeding; the characters are less dissimilar than first appearances would suggest. As the film gradually reveals the vulnerabilities the two men share, Sayad questions pervasive stereotypes in the representation of Algerian men.

As suggested above in relation to the stadium and its soccer fans, masculinity can't be isolated from the specific context where it is socially constructed and performed. The clandestine sheep fight arena is another highly coded masculine universe, with rules and expected competitive and aggressive behaviors. Samir is clearly supposed to occupy a dominant place in this universe. He seems to be known for selling good and reliable sheep. In almost every scene where Samir appears, he is bossing around either his son or the young men of his neighborhood. He is clearly the man who knows how to build a fence to keep sheep from escaping, the man who knows when to feed them and how to treat them. Sayad also films Samir stopping a fight between children in the street. As soon as Samir approaches, the boys stop fighting, as the scene demonstrates Samir's authority. Many of Samir's attributes correspond to those expected of a man in his position: he speaks few words, mainly to give orders, and he speaks in the broken voice of a heavy smoker, in some respects also an implicit attribute of manhood, especially in Algiers.

Samir is proud of his neighborhood, known in contemporary Algeria for its bravery and resistance to oppression. Bab El Oued which is also the privileged neighborhood of filmmaker Merzak Allouache who grew up and set most of his movies there—such as the now iconic *Omar Gatlato* (1976) and *Bab El Oued City* (1993)—is in fact the neighborhood where the social protests began in October 1988. Many of the estimated four hundred men and teenagers who were killed by the state in those days of protest are from this neighborhood. Thus, the famous and often-repeated slogan *"Bab El Oued El Chouhada"* ("the martyrs of Bab El Oued"). The neighborhood's inhabitants suffer from unemployment—as is true in many other places in Algiers and Algeria—but its reputation as a place of suffering was reinforced after severe flooding in November 2001 that claimed more than seven hundred victims. As Samir travels to Constantine to attend a fight, he describes the men with him as *ouled el Houma*—the sons of the neighborhood—and jokingly, adds, "those who kill and slaughter." Another sequence clearly references Islamist extremism, as Samir and his neighbors return from Constantine and celebrate the victory of their sheep by singing "La Carrière Al Qaïda," identifying their neighborhood as a place as powerful than Al Qaïda. Sayad makes the provocative choice of commenting on acts of great terror with irony and humor. Indeed, one cannot imagine terrorists in caves plotting against the west funded by Bin Laden.

Samir's behavior corresponds, most of the time, to a "will to conform" with a leading group's way of being. But as Connell explains, if hegemonic masculinity is marked by a successful claim to authority, then it is also subject to erosion or change when a new group challenges the reigning paradigm. We have a glimpse of this "erosion" when we watch Samir during scenes filmed in the south, buying sheep: his entire attitude, body language, and even his voice change drastically when he is not in a position of power. Leaving his neighborhood changes his social position. He must adjust to the codes of the sheep market, where he is an outsider, a simple buyer, and not the well-respected Samir from Bab El Oued. We can guess from Samir's interaction with a seller, with whom he uses a soft voice and negotiates calmly, that the codes governing Samir's daily life and universe are not relevant anymore in this market. Samir's powerlessness appears more evidently at the end of the documentary, where he acknowledges that power is actually in the hands of a few dominant men (those in power). He has little hope for his life and even for his son's future, offering in his own words the very definition of a patriarchal system in which only a few men dominate.

To better understand the prevalence of hegemonic masculinity, we need only look at how the filmmaker opposes Samir and Habib. Habib desperately tries to conform with what he considers the epitome of masculinity and success. He buys a sheep, El Bouq, and hopes to make a good fighter of him. Yet it appears quite early in the documentary that Habib, despite his efforts, will have difficulty attaining his goal. His nonchalance and even his slight chubbiness play against him, as Sayad cleverly insists on scenes where Habib feeds both himself and his sheep with candy and bread that are inappropriate for a future fighter. El Bouq ends up looking much like his owner, moving slowly and with some difficulty. The documentary thus tracks Habib as he enters a highly masculine world without being sufficiently armed to meet its rules and demands. There is a naïveté in his entire plan, as he thinks he is doing everything by the book when in fact he lacks the knowledge necessary to compete in the field. Habib's inadequacy in the space of masculine competition is also clear when he is on the phone trying to organize fights or when he tries to settle a feud with a neighbor who spoke ill of his sheep. Habib fails to assert his authority as he struggles to organize fights with men who seem equally unimpressed by him and his sheep. He finally creates several videos of El Bouq, which he posts on a Facebook page, hoping for answers and comments, but the buzz he is looking is never realized. When he calls the neighbor to confront him about the rumors Habib thinks he is spreading about his sheep, the conversation ends abruptly. The film doesn't clarify whether the neighbor hung up on him, or Habib didn't have enough credits on his phone to speak. Either alternative illustrates a powerlessness that is underscored by Habib's futile anger.

The scene where Habib's powerlessness is most obvious occurs when another sheep's owner comes to see El Bouq who is penned behind Habib's house. Habib wants to demonstrate that his sheep is ready to fight. The two men who arrive with their own fighting sheep have a completely different body language than Habib. They are more confident, more assertive. They are absolutely aware of the camera's presence and by trying hard to act naturally of course fail to do so. But soon the men forget about the camera and focus on what is at stake in the meeting. They criticize Habib for washing the sheep just before this small fight: the water has made the floor slippery, which is dangerous for the animals who can hurt each other inadvertently. The owners of the competing sheep observe El Bouq and end up telling Habib that he should shear the sheep. Habib answers that he doesn't have enough money, and then uncomfortably listens to a neighbor point out that he is not taking proper care of his sheep. To restore his lost authority, Habib adds that if he had enough money he would own at least sixteen sheep. The neighbor's mocking reply—"You can't handle one sheep, and you are talking about having sixteen!"—reestablishes Habib as the underdog, removing any possible doubt that the viewer would see him as anything but the loser in this exchange. El Bouq is not going to be a very competitive sheep, just as Habib is not a convincing contender for a powerful masculinity.

As he gets ready for El Bouq's first important fight, Habib giggles while being shaved, in a touching and funny scene that frames him as a teenager rather than the adult he aspires to be. But he lives fully his few seconds of fame and glory as he leads his sheep to the fight. His demeanor is totally different from that which he has displayed throughout the documentary. He acts confidently, he walks slowly with his head up, in the measured pace of a confident man, and he doesn't turn his eyes from the men who closely observe him. As the film's viewers have come to expect, El Bouq performs poorly. He seems scared of the other sheep and keeps returning to Habib instead of fighting. His failure is symbolically Habib's failure.

As *Des Moutons* concludes, neither Samir nor Habib is in a position of power. Each has tried to gain some agency in his life through a clandestine activity that can provide not only money but also social position and a positive image of their masculinity. But the film's overall message reveals their powerlessness on a larger scale; Sayad highlights their marginalization as he did with Djemil and Irhabi in his first documentary. Sayad also offers a telling observation of how violence, hegemonic masculinity, religiosity and marginalization are intertwined with complex characters. He refuses oversimplification and offers a view of Algerian men that is nuanced and complex.

My English Cousin (2019): Deconstructing a Dream

Sayad's most recent documentary, *My English Cousin* (2019), questions one of the most important myths in Algerian society: the dream of immigrating to Europe by any means possible, legal or not. Despairing of Algeria and its lack of opportunities and possibilities, most young Algerian men see Europe as an Eldorado of stable employment and life possibilities. As mentioned above, this theme was already present in Sayad's first documentary *Babor Casanova* (2015), evident in the title as well as the main characters' conversations. In *My English Cousin* (2019), Sayad expands his investigation, following his cousin Fahed who has settled in Grimsby, a small working-class town in England. Here, he deconstructs the myth of immigration as success story by showing what immigration has cost Fahed in both personal and familial terms.

Fahed settled illegally in England in 2000, living at first in London. Then, through a friend who lived in Grimsby, he discovered the town and decided it would be a nice place to live. He has married an English woman and at the time of the filming was working two jobs, one in a restaurant and the other in a bread factory. In our first look at Fahed, it seems he has successfully settled in England: he is no longer undocumented, he has a partner, and he is employed—which is not the case for all his male English friends. But Sayad decides to begin shooting his documentary in 2016, when his cousin had shared with him his desire to move back to Algeria. Sayad was interested in telling a migration story from the perspective of someone wanting to go back. Thus, when the documentary begins, Fahed is at a turning point of his life. He is unhappy in his marriage, and for the first time, he feels a need to return to Algeria. He misses his family and feels guilty for letting his mother live alone. The documentary investigates the reasons for this yearning and in the process, explores Fahed's present difficulties.

Sayad again uses an immersive point of view to make the spectator feel close to Fahed. As in his former documentaries, the camera follows the characters closely, and there is no voice-over to intervene between the viewer and the subjects. The documentary maker is even closer to his subject here because Karim Sayad and Fahed are first cousins and share a personal, emotional connection that is openly displayed in their on-camera interactions. Sayad appears on camera twice in the documentary. In the first instance, we see him helping his cousin get his car started, teasing Fahed about his inexperience as a driver. A second scene shows Sayad taking a picture of Fahed by the sea. The cameraman has ignored the director's instruction to cut and thus is able to capture a beautiful moment of complicity between the two cousins as they pose for a snapshot. The closeness—even intimacy—between the cousins allows the camera to be present even in Fahed's bedroom, where we see and hear Fahed asking his cousin Karim for the time when the alarm rings early in the morning. Sayad is apparently sleeping on the bedroom floor. Later in the documentary, we'll see the two men negotiating the time for which they need to set the alarm. This familial proximity allows Sayad to follow Fahed very closely in his daily life. Sayad's editing choices insist on Fahed's routine as he divides his time between work and home; he doesn't seem to socialize much or to pursue any hobby other than watching TV or videos on his phone. Fahed's loneliness is striking, and the viewer's empathy for him increases proportionally as Sayad's camera draws closer to his subject.

Sayad's immersive and ultra-close documentary style create the conditions for empathy and also for trust, a trust between subject and director that allows Fahed to reveal himself in all his vulnerabilities. He confides in his cousin, explains that he has ended up hating his way of life in England. Regarding his marriage, he is clearly conflicted: he is about to separate from his wife, but he feels remorse. Sayad's camera receives his confession and even operates as a witness to Fahed's good intentions and decency as before the camera he seems to promise—to Sayad and to the viewers—that he will try to stay friends with his wife and be there for her if she needs him. He acknowledges several times in the scene how much she has helped and supported him. The reasons for their separation are not very clear, though they seem to revolve around gender-role expectations. At one point, Fahed asks his cousin to describe what he would normally expect in a marriage, assuming the answer will be meals on the table and a clean house. The rhetorical questions he poses to his cousin—"If you get married wouldn't you be expecting food on the table?"—reveal his frustrations to his cousin and the film's viewers.

It's quite unusual for an Algerian man to explain—to himself or to others—why he is getting a divorce, since Algerian law and a patriarchal social structure make it easy for a husband to seek divorce. Once again, Sayad captures a man as he conveys a more complex masculinity than expected. Not only does Fahed show genuine feelings of guilt, doubt, and attachment, but his behavior is far from that expected of a so-called patriarch. Immigration and, most likely, a sense of isolation from his culture and community make Fahed compensate for what he can't find in his household. The film features several scenes in which Fahed himself cooks elaborate Algerian meals; Sayad insists on these moments, on the complexity of these meals, with close-ups on the plates. Cooking is, of course, an activity that is in theory reserved for women in Algeria—and Sayad takes the time to show that his English housemates are also surprised that Fahed is cooking. They congratulate him, jokingly declaring that he will be cooking every day, from now on. By cooking, working, and taking care of the house, Fahed is clearly conveying an image different from that of the hegemonic male not only in Algeria but within the British context.

It is, nevertheless, also clear that the documentary starts at a moment when Fahed's way of life in England—either with his wife or later in the documentary when he moves out to live with male housemates—is starting to weigh on him, and he is considering that a return to Algeria could bring him some answers and, more pragmatically, a new wife with whom he could find peace of mind. Unfortunately, and unsurprisingly, his trips to Algeria demonstrate even more strongly the violent disjunctions in space and time that characterize the experience of immigrants. Sayad follows his cousin through two trips to Algeria, during which Fahed tries to restore a lost sense of belonging and, perhaps, a masculinity that has been challenged and questioned during his years in England.

Fahed tries to regain his place in the family, assuming the role of patriarch. His father is absent from the picture, for reasons that the documentary never names—another interesting choice from the documentary maker, recalling Sayad's presentation of "Irhabi" in the earlier *Babor Casanova*. Whatever the reasons for his father's absence, Fahed's own decision to live abroad means he has failed to occupy fully this vacant patriarchal space. The only way he can do so now is by displaying economic power: bringing numerous gifts to his family and deciding who gets what, which takes place during a long and quite uncomfortable scene with his mother. Fahed lies on a bed while his mom actively goes through the gifts. This scene contrasts ironically with a pre-departure packing scene shot in Fahed's room in Grimsby, where he is struggling to make everything fit into his bags and worrying over likely excess baggage fees. His friend Gandhi watches incredulously as Fahed uses an unsophisticated (but efficient) technique to weigh his luggage—weighing body and luggage together, then subtracting his own weight to the one of his body and luggage. Gandhi is also surprised by the nature of the things Fahed is bringing with him to Algeria, genuinely asking if a safe can't be found in Algeria. In the packing scene, Fahed's economic power is invisible—his friend sees his massive bag as a display of folly, not of power—and that power materializes only briefly in Algeria. Sayad's editing, paralleling these scenes, beautifully highlights the problem of Fahed's hybrid identity.

Fahed's status as exile prevents him from regaining a fully respected position in the family, or at least keeps him from taking the patriarch's place. As he looks for a wife, the women around him keep questioning his decisions. When Sayad asks Fahed's mother what she thinks about her son's search, she expresses surprise that Fahed didn't meet with his fiancée; though she laconically answers that she can't tell her son what to do, since he is an adult, she implicitly criticizes his behavior and voices her powerlessness on the matter. But the feminine voice that most clearly second-guesses Fahed's choices is his aunt's. Here, for the first time in Sayad's documentary, a woman appears as a protagonist. It is not, perhaps, surprising that in his earlier two films women are absent, since each of these documentaries focuses on a male-dominated environment: clandestine sheep fights and soccer fandom.

In this familial documentary, by contrast, there is room for women, who feel confident enough to be filmed by a member of their family. And the aunt indeed expresses her opinions freely: she thinks that because Fahed has been living abroad for so many years, he has lost the skill and the knowledge necessary to navigate important matters like a marriage or starting a business in Algeria. Even if her intentions are affectionate, she undermines every decision her nephew makes about his marriage, asking who is his mysterious fiancée. She doubts the fiancée's intentions, criticizing the fiancée for failing to give presents to Fahed's mother, who had showered her with gifts. She implies several times to Fahed's face and even more when he is not present, that he has lost his mind, that he wants to get married at any price but lacks the capacity to secure a real marriage with a respectable woman.

Though the aunt states her admiration for Fahed's accomplishments, the broader effect of her participation in the documentary is to underscore that Fahed has lost his power as a man in Algeria. The aunt's speeches heighten the sense of displacement and isolation Fahed has been feeling since the beginning of the documentary. Through these challenges Sayad clearly deconstructs the myth not only of immigration as a pathway to happiness but also the myth of successful masculinity that none of his characters seems to reach in any of his documentaries. By disrupting many assumptions about masculinity in Algeria, Sayad builds a more generous view of Algerian men.

REFERENCES

Butler, Judith. "Performative Acts and Gender Constitution: An Essay in Phenomenology and Feminist Theory", *Theatre Journal*, Vol. 40, No. 4, Dec., 1988: 519-531.

Connell, Raewyn. *Masculinities.* Berkley: University of California Press, 2005.

Hussey, Andrew. *The French Intifada: The Long War Between France and Its Arabs.* London: Granta, 2014.

Khalil, Andrea. "The Myth of Masculinity in the Films of Merzak Allouache," Journal of North African Studies 12, no.3, 2007.

Inhorn, Marcia C. *The New Arab Man. Emergent Masculinities, Technologies, and Islam in the Middle East,* Princeton: Princeton University Press, 2012.

Niney, François. *Le documentaire et ses faux-semblants,* Paris: Klincksieck, 2009.

Sharpe, Mani. "Representing Masculinity in Postcolonial Algerian Cinema," Journal of North African Studies 20, no. 3 450–65, 2015.

CHAPTER 7

Conclusion

If I have focused on Algerian documentaries that have in common an immersive approach to the reality they film, it is important to recognize that many other documentaries have been created in Algeria since the end of the 1990s and many might well constitute manifestos for a genre still in progress. The omnipresence of "recent ruins" is a way to document a reality specific to the political context of Algeria. Such ruins can be seen as witness to the vestiges of the Civil War of the 1990s and of 60 years of authoritarian regime and also, to some extent, the more distant horrors of the colonial past. With the leitmotiv of "recent ruins," one cannot help but see a symbol of a national cinematography in crisis and the will for this new generation of filmmakers to constitute an aesthetic and a discourse that would be their own. The obsession in all of these documentaries with scrap heaps (*"ferrailles d'attente"*), vacant lots, or abandoned places reflects the state of Algerian cinema still under construction. The title of Djamel Kerkar's first feature documentary puts it eloquently: *Atlal* is a reference to an ancient Arab poetic genre which consists of standing in front of ruins and declaiming verse. The documentary *Chantier A (2013)* directed by Karim Loualiche, Lucie Dèche, and **Tarek Sami**, whose title is a reference to a construction site, opens with the beautiful image of a hand wiping a camera covered with raindrops. Both the title and the opening scene are a metaphor for a cinematography of hesitation, of trying to overcome the obstacles that hinder and slow down its progress.

© The Author(s), under exclusive license to Springer Nature Switzerland AG 2023
M. Belkaïd, *From Outlaw to Rebel*, Palgrave Studies in Arab Cinema, https://doi.org/10.1007/978-3-031-19157-2_7

And the obstacles are numerous. In December 2021, the Algerian Ministry of Culture announced that it was putting an end to the Fund for the Development of Arts, Technique, and the Cinematic Industry (FDATIC: *Fonds de Développement de l'Art, de la Technique et de l'Industrie Cinématographique*), confirming that there is, in Algeria, no real political commitment to relaunch production, distribution, and exhibition of films. Algerian filmmakers relied for a long time on the FDATIC, created in 1968 under the aegis of the Ministry of Culture and Arts, that regulates the cinematography sector in Algeria through its different institutions and commissions. The Fund was indeed responsible for providing financial aid for the production, post-production, writing, and rewriting of scripts, distribution, and exhibition of works in film. This decision leaves both established and rising filmmakers without any possibility for seeking public funds which were already scarce and difficult to obtain. Cinema professionals reacted to the decision by sending letters to the implicated authorities and by launching a campaign whose title, *tahya ya cinema* (long live cinema), paraphrases Mohammed Zinet's film title *Tahya ya Didou* (1971). They produced a protest video with scenes from iconic Algerian films, reminding all of the importance of Algerian filmmakers and citizens who create their own images about themselves and their country, rather than being constantly represented by "others." The absence of public funding opportunities will certainly render filmmaking more difficult than it has already been; filmmakers will have to find new strategies to finance, produce, and distribute their films. But the art of documentary-making is certainly not lost and will remain one of the avenues Algerian filmmakers will chose, maybe even more so, now that public funds are unreachable. As Hassen Ferhani often says, in times of adversity it's helpful to remember that a good film requires mostly a camera and a good idea.

In addition to shrinking funding opportunities, independent filmmakers will have to face other difficulties related to the political context that is, according to many analysts, more authoritarian than it has been during the Bouteflika years. As of this writing, more than 250 political prisoners across the country have been sentenced to jail or are awaiting trial, according to the Algerian detainees' website.[1] Freedom of speech is under attack with journalists imprisoned for articles they've published; some, like long-time journalist Ihsan El Kadi, stand accused of endangering the nation and reopening the wounds of the "national tragedy" as the Civil war of the

---

[1] https://www.algerian-detainees.org. Accessed June 14, 2022.

1990s is called by the current regime. *Liberté*, one of the francophone newspapers born during the democratic opening of the late 1980s, was closed by its new owner Issad Rabrab, who is close to the Algerian power circle. The ministry of culture announced in April 2022 the creation of a reading commission that will be charged with handling filming authorizations, a decision interpreted by many filmmakers as barely disguised censorship and a new way to control cinematographic work. Throughout all my conversations with Algerian filmmakers, producers, and technicians, all involved are aware of the obstacles the industry faces and that the coming years are going to be more and more challenging for filmmakers.

And yet, to borrow the words of Algerian film critic Mouny Berrah that inspired this book's title, Algerian documentary that was born an outlaw during the Algerian War of Independence will most probably remain a rebel, despite the difficulties and obstacles. In addition to the crucial work of Habiba Djahnine in training emerging documentary makers (Chap. 2), a new generation of filmmakers is also involved in facilitating access for aspiring filmmakers and producers, to funding sources, savoir-faire, and technologies. Drifa Mezenner, a documentary maker herself, launched in 2018 her own production house and platform called *Tahya Cinema* (Long live cinema) that aspires to support filmmakers in their endeavors by organizing workshops, encouraging networking, and facilitating encounters between cinema professionals. In the city of Setif, filmmaker Yanis Koussim has also created PLATEAU 19 collective, an organization partnered with the nonprofit arts organization Film Independent based in Los Angeles and whose mission is to encourage creative independence in visual storytelling.[2] Koussim has organized workshops for Algerian filmmakers and producers since 2020.

Even if the future seems grim for Algerian cinema, many photographers and filmmakers are at work documenting contemporary Algeria. Amine Kabbès, Walid Sahraoui, Drifa Mezenner, Bahia Benchikh El Fegoun, and photographer Fethi Sahraoui[3] are currently filming documentaries. In 2018, Amine Kabbès decided to film the day-to-day campaign of activist Fethi Gharès, for the presidential election. During the film's shooting, the *Hirak* movement started in February 2019, against Bouteflika's candidacy and more broadly against the Algerian regime. The film follows Fethi

[2] https://www.filmindependent.org.
[3] See Fethi Sahraoui's photographic work https://fethisahraoui.net. Accessed June 19, 2022.

Gharès during these tumultuous times, until his imprisonment in June 2021, having been accused of insulting the head of state. Kabbès of course didn't ask for public funds for his film and no one can tell if or when his documentary will be screened in Algeria. He must negotiate with obstacles and implicit threats of censorship. He is nevertheless currently finishing the editing of his documentary that was selected at the Swiss Festival *Visions du Réel*, which provides invaluable postproduction mentorship and funding. This example, as many others, shows how much documentary in Algeria and in the region is more relevant and perhaps more powerful than ever.

After the hope born during the Hirak, Algeria is facing new political difficulties as are its neighbors. After the 2011 revolution, Tunisians elected the Assembly of the Representatives of the People on October 26, 2014, and a new President in 2014 and again in 2019, thus ending a crucial and founding stage in the transition begun after the uprising of 2010–2011. Now a new phase is unfolding in which the challenge is to test the new institutions and principles provided for in the 2014 Constitution which are meant to establish a democratic political regime. This constitution is currently threatened by President Kaïs Saied who calls for a new one, having dissolved the Assembly in July 2021. Morocco did not witness the same level of protest as in 1988 and 2019 Algeria or in 2011 Tunisia. Regardless, the wave of protests in Morocco in 2011 is not to be taken lightly. It suggests that the measures put in place, including a new constitution and some devolution of power, are insufficient to address the deep economic and political challenges facing Moroccans. Since the end of the 1980s, not only Algeria but also Tunisia and Morocco and other countries of the region are facing important political and social changes. I hope to have shown in this book how Independent Algerian cinema is documenting their plight and how documentary is a producer and product of progressive social and political movements.

In Tunisia and Morocco, creative documentary has remained a minor and marginal genre in the first decades after the independence, attracting fewer viewers than fiction, not always having been able to develop freely under authoritarian regimes. Indeed, the subjects filmed were often afraid to express themselves in front of a camera and as in Algeria, a barely concealed institutionalized censorship was continuously at play. During the 2000s, as Zine El-Abidine Ben Ali's regime in Tunisia both hardened and lost momentum, Tunisian filmmakers began to explore new thematic and aesthetic avenues thanks to technological innovations, such as the digital camera. Thus, from the early 2000s, documentaries until then unthinkable under an authoritarian regime, were produced. *Raïs Labhar* (2002) by Hichem Ben Ammar, winner in 2002 at the *Journées Cinématographiques de Carthage*, documents the harshness of life in the tuna fishing industry. In *VHS Kahloucha* (2008), Nejib Belkhadi follows the tribulations of Moncef Kahloucha who, as an amateur and with his own means, reconstructs classic films such as *Tarzan*. The film invites reflection on the power of image and cinema. Set in the poor neighborhood of Kazmet in the city of Sousse, *VHS Kahloucha* conveys how Ben Ali's regime can no longer maintain the façade of an alleged economic and cultural miracle. The revolution of 2011 has given rise to an increasing number of documentaries. As the country witnessed tremendous political and social transformation, Hend Boujemaa directed *C'était mieux demain* (2012) that follows a homeless women named Aïda before and after the revolution, in her quest for an appartement for her and her son. In *Babylon* (2012), while anger is mounting in Tunis and all the cameras are focused on the capital, it is in a refugee camp on the Tunisian-Libyan border that Ismaël, Youssef Chebbi, and Ala Eddine Slim choose to set their cameras. These filmmakers were driven by the desire to bear witness to the events happening in the country. There is in all these choices a willingness to prohibit the media, or any dominant discourse from dictating the content and location of the images they produce.

After years of dictatorship, directors have started to freely explore the blind spots of a Tunisia whose idyllic image has been formatted by official speeches and national and foreign media. Many of these documentaries are the result of several years of work. The directors are indeed aware of exploring universes that have rarely been shown on screen and they take the necessary time to get to know them better. This work of immersion, a hallmark of not only Algerian but also of many North African documentaries, invites the viewer into a sensory and auditory experience and takes the risk of shocking spectators by showing what is usually considered taboo. Hamza Ouini filmed his two documentaries simultaneously in Mohammedia, his hometown south of Tunis. *El Gort* (2014) took seven years to be completed and follows Mohamed and Khaïri, two workers of precarious status in the hay trade. *El Medestansi* (2020) narrates 12 years of the life of Mehrez Taher, a dancer and actor addicted to gambling and alcohol. Nasredine Shili offers with *Subutex* (2018) a documentary that films the intimate life of two homosexuals and drug addicts, living clandestinely in a hammam in the neighborhood of Bab El Jdid, in Tunis. In *Les*

Voix de Kasserine (2016), Olfa Lamloum and Michel Tabet explore a marginalized region of the country that is awaiting economical improvements after the revolution. In *La Voie normale* (2018), Erige Sehiri follows the difficulties faced by Tunisian railway workers, while *Maudit soit le phosphate* (2012) by Sami Tlili documents the revolts that happened in 2008 in the region of Redeyef, related to the mining industry. In 2019, Tlili filmed *Sur la transversale*, which focuses on the year 1978 in Tunisia, with a showdown between the regime of Habib Bourguiba and the workers union (UGTT) led by Habib Achour. More conventional, this documentary tackles topics like football, trade unionism, and politics, and questions the last years of Bourguiba's reign.

As for Morocco, creative documentaries remained almost non-existent for a long time, as Hicham Falah, general delegate of the International Documentary Film Festival (Fidadoc) in Agadir pointed out in 2017: "Ten years ago, documentaries were practically absent from our audiovisual landscape. Except for a few individuals, especially Moroccans based abroad, the practice and distribution of documentary cinema had disappeared in Morocco."[4] This rarity can be explained by structural reasons related to financing films, but also by political ones: the Moroccan authorities controlled the public discourse very closely. Leila Kilani had taken advantage of the accession of Mohamed VI to the throne in 1999, to begin a documentary work on the abuses committed during the reign of his father Hassan II, with *Nos lieux interdits* (2008). The film follows four families over three years as they suffer from violence during the Hassan II reign. But with the kingdom returning to more speech control in the last decade, documentaries have since become rare. We should nevertheless point out the work of Hind Bensari, Nadir Bouhmouch, and Dalila Ennadre who are clearly proponents of a militant cinema. Hind Bensari's first documentary, *475: Trêve de silence*, denounces an article of law which stipulates that rape is punishable by several years in prison, unless the perpetuator marries his victim. This film played an important part in the protest movement which ended up obtaining the repeal of the article in question. Hind Bensari's second documentary, *We could be heroes* (2018), follows for more than two years the journey of two Moroccan athletes who are preparing for the 2016 Paralympic Games. Azzedine, celebrated by national media, returns with a gold medal but without the salary

---

[4] Dorothée Myriam Kellou, « La Création documentaire au Maroc et en Afrique a totalement explosé », *Le Monde*, le 26 juin, 2018. [my translation].

promised by the Moroccan authorities. Organizing a sit-in in Rabat, he will end up in police custody, accused of disrupting public order for having demonstrated for his rights. Nadir Bouhmouch, in *Amussu* (2019) portrays the fight in the village of Imider, which for eight years has been resisting peacefully the exploitation of a large mine which diverts drinkable water and dries up the surrounding land. Dalila Ennadre, who passed away in 2020, relentlessly gave voice to silenced women activists in *Une Heroïne sans gloire* (2004) and *Je voudrais vous raconter* (2005), and a prostitute during the colonization in *J'ai tant aimé* (2008). These directors document social and territorial inequalities and show a Morocco fighting for social and political change.

Independent North African Cinema is admittedly not one that explores spaces and territories through a free and joyful wandering but rather show the real and symbolic paralysis in which characters and their countries are locked. A prime example is Omar Belhouchet running on his treadmill in Bensmaïl's documentary *Contre-pouvoirs* (Chap. 3); his mobility is an illusion because of the situation of political or economic crisis which confines journalists but also filmmakers in a delimited space in which they constantly need to negotiate freedom and dissidence. And what about the roundabout in Youcef's head which gave its title to Hassen Ferhani's documentary, *Dans ma tête un rondpoint* (Chap. 4)? The image speaks for itself and shows a subject that goes around in circles and is unable to project himself into the future. He too, like many others, sees no other alternatives than theft, suicide, or illegal emigration. Ismaël, Youssef Chebbi and Ala Eddine Slim in *Babylon* (2012) use the device of accelerating a series of images of the passers-by who cross into the refugee camp to show that mobility is factitious, not only because of the situation of political or economic crisis which confines the inhabitants of Algiers or the refugees of the camp of Choucha but also in a more symbolic way. One easily surmises that these young directors themselves and their works have trouble finding their place and circulating freely. One cannot help but think of the visibility of documentaries within an Algerian and North African cinematographic production that is already so compromised and discrete. Of course, many of these documentaries have been awarded prizes at numerous international festivals, but rare are the documentaries that succeed in attracting the attention of spectators, the media, and academics. These films share with their subjects, an intrinsic marginality.

They nevertheless find ways to circulate in Festivals but also in universities in the US and Europe. In April 2022, Algerian filmmaker Hassen

Ferhani was invited to Yale University to screen his last feature documentary, *143 rue du désert* (Chap. 4). The screening was part of a symposium and was present under the rubric of "The Desert Futures Collective," a network of scholars, activists, and artists whose shared goal is "to chart new paradigms for interdisciplinary humanities scholarship through a comparative focus on the poetics and politics of desert spaces." The symposium opened with another documentary *At(h)ome* by French filmmaker Elisabeth Leuvrey. In this film, Leuvrey and Bruno Hadjih, an Algerian photographer, explore the irradiated desert zone of In Eker and follow the path of the so-called Béryl incident, one of the 17 nuclear experiments conducted by France in the Algerian Sahara between 1960 and 1966. Both documentaries explore the same space but with different perspectives. If in Ferhani's film the colonial past is not central, Leuvrey's film that focuses clearly on the traces left by colonialism in Algeria and on geographical scars that question the responsibility of the French and Algerian state. Both films are equally important to understanding contemporary Algeria. Interestingly, the discussion that followed both films engaged different scholars. While Leuvrey's film entailed an interdisciplinary conversation, Ferhani's was mainly discussed as a cinematographic object, as beautiful and compelling as it is. Is it because France is absent from the film that makes it a challenging or unusual object of analysis through an interdisciplinary perspective? While attending this engaging conference at the last stages of writing this book, it became clear to me that my work is born from the willingness to analyze the work of contemporary Algerian filmmaker like Hassen Ferhani, Malek Bensmaïl, and others, not only as cinematographic objects but also as cultural productions that allow for a better understanding of contemporary Algeria. I wanted to explore what Algerian cultural productions were telling us about the country, and not systematically through the lens of colonial past and trauma. Their diagnosis on contemporary Algeria is nuanced, but they are mainly focused on the challenges, responsibilities, and failures of the Algerian state after the independence.

Academics often tend to forget that while the colonial past is still impacting the country, other forces are at play in present day Algeria. Algerian cinema and cultural productions in general have a lot to offer for anyone trying to understand a sixty-year-old independent nation, still finding its way toward freedom and democracy. They provide ways to explore how Algerians live today, what obstacles they are up against, what their dreams and hopes are, and how they can achieve what some protesters during the *Hirak* movement called a "second independence," that would free the country from authoritarianism and a corrupt regime.

This book does not explore all the potential of North African documentaries. Far from it. It started its journey through Algerian documentary with *La Chine est encore loin*, in the village of Ghassira, one of the places where the Algerian War of Independence started. In a striking scene, an inhabitant of the village complains about the difficulty of daily life in Ghassira. He invites Malek Bensmaïl to film artisanal pottery and jewelry that belonged to his mother, a heritage he is proud of and promotes. The filmmaker indulges him and marvels at the intrinsic beauty and the past and present political significance of the landscapes that surround them. Both remind us that all these places must be explored and seen. Algerian and North African cultural productions—concerned with the colonial past or not—deserve this attention.

FILMOGRAPHY

143 rue du désert (Hassen Ferhani, 2019), 104 mins.
475 : Trêve de silence (Hind Bensari, 2013), 43 mins.
Abdelkader (Salem Brahimi, 2014), 93 mins.
Africa is back (Salem Brahimi 2010), 93 mins.
Afric Hotel (Hassen Ferhani, Nabil Djedouani, 2010), 54 mins.
Algérie en flammes (René Vautier, 1958), 22 mins.
Algérie la vie quand même (Djamila Sahraoui, 1998), 52 mins.
L'Algérie la vie toujours (Djamila Sahraoui, 2001), 50 mins.
Algériennes 30 ans après (Ahmed Lallem, 1995), 52 mins.
Algérie (s) (Malek Bensmaïl, Thierry Leclère, 2002), 160 mins.
Aliénations (Malek Bensmaïl, 2004), 105 mins.
A Mansourah, tu nous as séparés (Dorothée Myriam Kellou, 2019), 71 mins.
Amussu (Nadir Bouhmouch, 2019), 100 mins.
L'Après octobre (Merzak Allouache, 1988), 88 mins.
Arezki, l'indigène (Djamel Bendeddouche, 2007), 90 mins.
At(h)ome (Elisabeth Leuvrey, 2016), 53 mins.
Atlal (Djamel Kerkar, 2017), 100 mins.
Archipel (Djamel Kerkar, 2012), 13 mins
L'Aube des damnés (Ahmed Rachedi, 1965), 100 mins.
Autrement citoyens (Habiba Djahnine, 2008), 52 mins.
Avant de franchir la ligne d'horizon (Habiba Djahnine, 2011), 64 mins.
Bab El Oued City (Merzak Allouache, 1994), 93mins.

© The Author(s), under exclusive license to Springer Nature
Switzerland AG 2023
M. Belkaïd, *From Outlaw to Rebel*, Palgrave Studies in Arab
Cinema, https://doi.org/10.1007/978-3-031-19157-2

Babor Casanova (Karim Sayad, 2015), 35 mins.
Les Baies d'Alger (Hassen Ferhani, 2006), 14 mins.
Babylon (Ismaël, Youssef Chebbi and Ala Eddine Slim, 2012), 119 mins.
Barberouuse (Hadj Rahim, 1982), 100 mins.
Barberousse mes soeurs, (Hassan Bouabdallah, 1985), 62 mins.
La Bataille d'Alger (Gillo Pontecorvo, 1965), 121 mins.
La Bataille d'Alger, l'empreinte (Cheikh Djemai, 2018), 52 mins.
La Bataille d'Alger. Un film dans l'histoire (Malek Bensmaïl, 2017), 117 mins.
Bla Cinema (Lamine Ammar Khodja, 2014), 82 mins.
Boudiaf un espoir assassiné (Malek Bensmaïl, 1999), 58 mins.
C'était mieux demain (Hend Boujemaa, 2012), 74 mins.
La Clôture (Tariq Teguia, 2002), 23 mins.
Chantier A (Lucie Dèche, Karim Loualiche, Tarek Sami, 2013), 104 mins.
Le Charbonnier (Mohammed Bouamari, 1972), 97 mins.
La Chine est encore loin (Malek Bensmaïl, 2008), 120 mins.
Chroniques des années de braise (Mohamed Lakhdar Hamina, 1974), 177 mins.
Le Clandestin (Benamar Bakhti, 1991), 103 mins.
La Coline oubliée (Abderhamne Bouguermouh, 1996), 90 mins.
Combien je vous aime (Azzedine Meddour, 1985), 105 mins.
Contre-pouvoirs (Malek Bensmaïl, 2015), 97 mins.
Le Cri des hommes (Okacha Touita, 1990), 100 mins.
Dans le feu hier et aujourd'hui (Okacha Touita, 1999), 52 mins.
Dans ma tête un rondpoint (Hassen Ferhani, 2015), 100 mins.
Djazairouna (René Vautier, Djamel-Eddine Chanderli, Mohamed Lakhdar Hamina and Pierre Chaulet, 1961), 18 mins.
Décembre (Mohamed Lakhdar Hamina, 1972), 95 mins.
Des moutons et des hommes (Karim Sayad, 2017), 78 mins.
Elles (Ahmed Lallem, 1967), 22 mins.
El Gort (Hamza Ouini, 2014), 77 mins.
El Medestansi (Hamza Ouini, 2020), 114 mins.
Et Maintenant ils peuvent venir (Salem Brahimi, 2015), 95 mins.
L'Évasion de Hassen Terro (Mustapha Badie, 1974), 115 mins.
Fadhma N'Soumer (Belkacem Hadjadj, 2013), 110 mins.
Fama, une héroïne sans gloire (Dalila Ennadre, 2004), 52 mins.
Femmes en mouvement (Merzak Allouache, 1989), 52 mins.
Ferraille d'attente (Tariq Teguia, 1998), 7 mins.
Festival Panafricain d'Alger 1969 (William Klein, 1969), 112 mins.

Le Fort des fous (Narimane Mari, 2017), 150 mins.

Fragments de rêve (Bahia Bencheikh El Fegoun, 2017), 75 mins.

Les Fusils de la liberté (Djamel Chanderli, Mohamed Lakhdar Hamina, 1962), 27 mins.

Le Grand Jeu (Malek Bensmaïl, 2005), 90 mins.

Guerres secrètes du FLN en France (Malek Bensmaïl 2012),

Hassan Niyya (Ghaouti Bendeddouche, 1988), 90 mins.

Hassan Taxi (Slim Riad, 1982), 110 mins.

Hassan Terro (Mohamed Lakhdar Hamina, 1968), 90 mins.

J'ai huit ans (Yann Le Masson et Olga Poliakoff, 1961), 9 mins.

J'ai habité l'absence deux fois (Drifa Mzener, 2011), 23 mins.

J'ai tant aimé (Dalila Ennadre, 2008), 50 mins.

Janitou, (Amine Hattou, 2019), 81 mins.

Jean Genet, notre père des fleurs (Dalila Ennadre, 2020), 60 mins.

Je voudrais vous raconter (Dalila Ennadre, 2005), 50 mins.

Krim Belkacem (Ahmed Rachedi, 2012), 180 mins.

Lettre à ma soeur (Habiba Djahnine, 2008), 68 mins.

Leur Algérie (Lina Soualem, 2020), 82 mins.

Lotfi (Ahmed Rachedi, 2015), 170 mins.

Loubia Hamra (Narimane Mari, 2013), 80 mins.

Mostefa Ben Boulaïd (Ahmed Rachedi, 2008), 163 mins.

My English Cousin (Karim Sayad 2019), 82 mins.

Nar (Meriem Bouakaz Achour, 2019), 52 mins.

Omar Gatlato (Merzak Allouache, 1979), 90 mins.

L'Oued, l'oued, (Abdenour Zahzah, 2013), 86 mins.

*Les mains libres (*Ennio Lorenzini, *1964)*, 50 mins.

Maudit soit le phosphate (Sami Tlili, 2012), 85 mins.

La montagne de Baya (Azzedine Meddour, 1997), 116 mins.

La moitié du ciel d'Allah (Djamila Sahraoui, 1995), 50 mins.

Nos lieux interdits (Leila Kilani, 2008), 105 mins.

La Nouba des femmes du Mont Chenoua (Assia Djebar, 1978), 115 mins.

Peuple en marche (René Vautier, 1963), 50 mins.

La promesse de juillet (Mohamed Lakhdar Hamina, 1963)

L'Opium et le bâton (Ahmed Rachedi,1969), 135 mins.

Patrouille à l'est (Amar Laskri, 1971), 115 mins.

Raïs Labhar (Hichem Ben Ammar, 2002), 45 mins.

Les Remparts d'argile (Jean-Louis Bertucelli, 1970), 80 mins.

Le Rescapé (Okacha Touita, 1986), 80 mins.

Retour à la montagne (Habiba Djahnine, 2010), 50 mins.

Le roman algérien (Katia Kameli, 2016), 95 mins.

Les Sacrifiés (Okacha Touita 1982), 100 mins.

Sakiet Sidi Youcef (Pierre Clément et René Vautier,1958),

Samir dans la Poussière (Mohamed Ouzine, 2015), 59 mins.

Subutex (Nasredine Shili, 2018), 102 mins.

Sur la transversale (Sami Tlili, 2019), 96 mins.

Tarzan, Don Quichotte et nous (Hassen Ferhani 2013), 19 mins.

Tahya ya Didou (Mohamed Zinet,1971), 76 mins.

Toute l'Algérie du Monde (2021)

Une si jeune paix (Jacques Charby 1964), 90 mins.

Un seul acteur le peuple (René Vautier1962), 14 mins.

Le Vent des Aurès (Mohamed Lakhdar Hamina,1967), 95mins.

VHS Kahloucha (Nejib Belkhadi, 2008), 80 mins.

La Voie (Mohamed Slim Riad 1968), 95 mins.

La Voie normale (Erige Sehiri, 2018), 75 mins.

Les Voix de Kasserine (Olfa Lamloum, Michel Tabet, 2017), 53 mins.

Le Vol du 104 (Hassen Ferhani, 2008), 14 mins.

Vote Off (Fayçal Hammoum, 2017), 82 mins.

We could be heroes (Hind Bensari, 2018), 80 mins.

Youssef. La légende du septième dormant (Mohamed Chouikh,1993),105 mins.

La Zerda ou les chants de l'oubli (Assia Djebar, 1982), 60 mins.

INDEX[1]

[1] Note: Page numbers followed by 'n' refer to notes.

© The Author(s), under exclusive license to Springer Nature Switzerland AG 2023
M. Belkaïd, *From Outlaw to Rebel*, Palgrave Studies in Arab Cinema, https://doi.org/10.1007/978-3-031-19157-2

CPSIA information can be obtained
at www.ICGtesting.com
Printed in the USA
LVHW050017050223
738687LV00005B/99

9 783031 191565